Designed and published by the
Wales Tourist Board, Brunel House,
2 Fitzalan Road, Cardiff CF2 1UY.
Written by Roger Thomas Freelance Services.
Typesetting by Keith James Design Associates.
Colour reproduction by Scanagraphics Ltd.
Printed by A. McLay & Co.
Copyright © 1997 Wales Tourist Board.
ISBN 1 85013 074 4

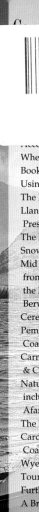

Llyn Nantlle, Snowdonia

Llanberis Lake Railway

Accommodation Plus ...

This is more than an accommodation guide. It's a complete holiday planner, with information on Wales's countryside and coastline, its national parks and 'Areas of Outstanding Natural Beauty', its countless castles, craft workshops and attractions.

The great outdoors

Wales's fresh, green surroundings are an increasingly prized asset. It's a pleasant surprise to discover, in this day and age, that you can drive uninterrupted all the way from South to North Wales through a landscape of hills and mountains. Or that you can walk for almost 200 miles along a coast path in Pembrokeshire with only the seabirds for company.

There are no less than three national parks here – the Brecon Beacons, Pembrokeshire Coast and Snowdonia. There are even more official 'Areas of Outstanding Beauty' – the Clwydian Range, Gower Peninsula, Isle of Anglesey, Llŷn Peninsula and Wye Valley. And 40 per cent of Wales's 750-mile seashore has been designated as untouched Heritage Coast.

Attractions and activities

This great natural beauty is a backcloth for all kinds of things to see and do. Wales's rich history is reflected in atmospheric medieval castles and walled towns. Its vibrant artistic and cultural life is expressed at folk festivals and craft workshops.

The country is a stimulating mix of traditional and innovative – old slate caverns have been revitalised as tourist attractions, there are narrow-gauge railways and a unique 'village of the future' dedicated to conservation. And on the activities front, Wales offers everything from walking to watersports, pony trekking to mountain biking.

White wat rafting, Ri♦ Treweryn, Bala

2

Three Cliffs Bay, Gower

Pen-y-fan, Brecon Beacons National Park

Green Wales

Point to any part of Wales on the map and you're likely to locate beautiful surroundings – rugged Snowdonia in the north, perhaps, or the high, wild country of the Cambrian Mountains in Mid Wales, or the grassy slopes of the Brecon Beacons in the south.

Wales is green from top to bottom. The quality of its environment is something special – and it intends to keep it this way. There's a wealth of precious, protected places in Wales's many national parks and nature reserves, 'Areas of Outstanding Natural Beauty' and country parks.

Snowdonia and the Brecon Beacons

These two national parks are very different in character. Snowdonia is a dramatic jumble of rocky outcrops, tumbling rivers, brooding moors and deep, wooded valleys. The Brecon Beacons, in contrast, are smooth, grassy and open, offering a rare sense of space and freedom.

The Snowdonia National Park takes its name from Snowdon, the highest mountain in England and Wales. It's a huge area of 845 square miles, extending southwards all the way to Machynlleth. The 519-square-mile Brecon Beacons National Park also covers a lot of ground, from the Wales/England border almost as far as Swansea.

Wild Wales, verdant vales

Wales's undisturbed rural heartlands lie in Mid Wales, an area of rolling border country, lakes and mountains. When people speak of 'Wild Wales' they refer to the remote wildernesses of Plynlimon and the Cambrian Mountains, or the silent hills and marshlands around Tregaron where the rare red kite has made its home, or the spectacular old drover's road that climbs across the 'roof of Wales' to Abergwesyn.

Wales also has its pastoral, sheltered side along valleys such as the lovely vales of Conwy and Clwyd in the north, and the Teifi and Towy in the south.

Areas of outstanding beauty

Possibly the loveliest valley of them all is the Wye Valley, an 'Area of Outstanding Natural Beauty' which runs northwards from Chepstow to Monmouth through thickly wooded hillsides. And in North Wales there's another AONB – the Clwydian Range, an exhilarating line of rounded hills standing guard over green border country and the rich farmlands of the Vale of Clwyd.

Craig-goch Reservoir, Elan Valley

Coasting Along

Wales's 750-mile coastline has something for everyone – lively resorts and secluded coves, salty old fishing villages and modern marinas, popular beaches and remote bays.

Tenby

Beside the seaside

For entertainment-packed seaside holidays, there's the sandy North Wales coast with its string of attractive resorts – elegant Llandudno (where you'll find Wales's best selection of hotels and guest houses) and the colourful, happy-go-lucky appeal of Colwyn Bay, Rhyl and Prestatyn.

Along the Mid Wales coast, Aberystwyth is an attractive mix of Victorian and modern influences. Barmouth and Tywyn, with their fine beaches and mountain-backed settings, are also popular spots, while picturesque Aberdovey attracts sailors as well as holidaymakers.

South Wales's long coastline offers everything from all the fun of the fair at Barry Island and Porthcawl to stylish Saundersfoot and Georgian Tenby.

Away from it all

Wales's national parklands, 'Areas of Outstanding Natural Beauty' and Heritage Coast are made for the quieter style of seaside holiday. The Isle of Anglesey, fringed with vast dunes, rocky promontories and beaches, is dotted with charming little resorts like Rhosneigr, Beaumaris and Benllech.

Anglesey and the Llŷn Peninsula are official AONBs. Along the Llŷn's spectacular shores you'll discover more splendid, secluded beaches, towering cliff scenery, and pretty places to stay such as Abersoch, Criccieth and Nefyn.

There's a grand sweep of coastline, from north to south, along Cardigan Bay. Here, you can get lost amongst the dunes of Shell Island near Harlech, or explore the coves and grassy headlands of Ceredigion's Heritage Coast (don't miss Mwnt, a little jewel, or the quaysides at New Quay and Aberaeron).

Pembrokeshire is another – and bigger – jewel. The Pembrokeshire Coast National Park is one of Europe's finest stretches of coastal natural beauty. Wherever you chose – Newport, Fishguard or St David's in the north, Newgale, Broad Haven or Dale in the west, Tenby or Saundersfoot in the south – you'll be amongst breathtaking coastal scenery.

There's more great beauty along the endless sands of Carmarthen Bay where Dylan Thomas sought his inspiration, and the magnificent Gower Peninsula. Gower's sheltered sandy bays and sea-cliffs enjoy a special status – the peninsula was the first part of Britain to be declared an 'Area of Outstanding Natural Beauty'.

Llanddwyn Island, Isle of Anglesey

An Eventful Year

Although it's a bit of a cliché to say the Welsh love to sing, this one happens to be true. A love of music is part of a rich cultural life which is expressed in festivals, performances and events throughout Wales. Venues such as Cardiff's St David's Hall, Theatr Clwyd in Mold and the North Wales Theatre in Llandudno stage everything from West End productions to comedy, classical music to pop. The prestigious Cardiff Singer of the World competition, at which Bryn Terfel first came to prominence, takes place at St David's Hall in June.

Wales's most traditional cultural gathering is the *eisteddfod* (which means 'sitting together'). In addition to the many eisteddfodau held here, you can listen to world-class jazz at Brecon and Llangollen, mix with international literary stars at Hay-on-Wye, enjoy a colourful countryside jamboree at Builth Wells, or take a trip back to Victorian times at Llandrindod Wells.

Here, we've listed just some of the events on offer, beginning with the main activities. More details of 1997 events are contained in a series of quarterly Events leaflets, available free from: Wales Tourist Board, Davis Street, Cardiff CF1 2FU.

MAJOR EVENTS 1997

22 February - 1 November
The Last Invasion of Britain Bicentenary

The last invasion of British soil took place in Pembrokeshire in 1797. Many events have been planned in West Wales to mark this historic occasion. Tel: (01348) 874997

End of May - end of December
Mid Wales Festival of the Countryside

A festival which brings together over 500 events taking place throughout beautiful Mid Wales - bird-watching, guided walks, arts and crafts, sheepdog trials, farm and garden visits. David Bellamy, a keen supporter, has called it 'the role model for sustainable tourism'. Tel: (01686) 625384

23 May - 1 June
Hay Festival of Literature

Hay-on-Wye, the borderland 'town of books', provides an ideal setting for this literary festival with an international reputation. Attracts leading writers, poets and celebrities. Tel: (01497) 821217

8-13 July
Llangollen International Musical Eisteddfod

A colourful, cosmopolitan gathering of singers and dancers from all over the world perform in the beautiful little town of Llangollen. A unique festival first held in 1947 to help heal the wounds of war by bringing the peoples of the world together. Tel: (01978) 860236

21-24 July
Royal Welsh Show

Four days of fascination and entertainment at a show that attracts a wide audience to Builth Wells, not just from the farming community but from all walks of life. One of Wales's premier events, held in the heart of the country, covering all aspects of agriculture - and a lot more besides. Tel: (01982) 553683

2-9 August
Royal National Eisteddfod

Wales's most important cultural gathering, dating back to 1176, and held at a different venue each year. A festival dedicated to Welsh, Britain's oldest living language, with competitions, choirs, concerts, stands and exhibitions. Translation facilities available. This year's event will be held at Bala. Tel: (01222) 763777

8-10 August
Brecon Jazz

The streets of Brecon come alive with the sounds of summer jazz. A great three-day international festival with a wonderful atmosphere, which attracts the top names from the world of jazz. Over 80 concerts by bands and solo artists held throughout the town, both indoors and in the open air. Tel: (01874) 625557

16-24 August
Llandrindod Wells Victorian Festival

The Mid Wales spa town of Llandrindod Wells celebrates its Victorian past. The festival includes street theatre, walks, talks, drama, exhibitions and music - all with a Victorian flavour. Tel: (01597) 823441

1997 Events for Everyone

1 February
Wales v Ireland Rugby International, Cardiff Arms Park

1 March
St David's Day Concert, St David's Hall, Cardiff

7-9 March
Folk Weekend, Llanwrtyd Wells

8 March
Festival of Male Voice Praise, Brangwyn Hall, Swansea

International Women's Day Celebration, County Hall, Cardiff Bay

15 March
Wales v England Rugby International, Cardiff Arms Park

26 March
Conwy Seed Fair

29-31 March
Welsh Camping and Caravanning Show, Royal Welsh Showground, Builth Wells

2-5 May
Landsker Walking Festival, Narberth

3-9 May
Bodedern and District Festival

4 May
Welsh Festival of Dressage, Usk Showground

5-10 May
Llandrindod Wells Drama Festival

9-11 May
Llangollen International Jazz Festival

9-25 May
Wrexham Arts Festival

24-31 May
Hay Children's Festival of the Arts

24 May - 1 June
St David's Cathedral Festival

25-26 May
City and County of Swansea Show

26-31 May
Urdd National Eisteddfod (Youth Eisteddfod), Cross Keys, nr Caerphilly

7 June
Llangollen Choral Festival

14 June
Man versus Horse Marathon, Llanwrtyd Wells

14 - 20 June
Barmouth to Fort William Three Peaks Yacht Race

15 - 21 June
Cardiff Singer of the World, St David's Hall

18 - 22
Criccieth Festival of Music and the Arts

20 - 22 June
Craft Show in the Garden, Erddig, Wrexham

Gŵyl Ifan - Welsh Folk Dancing Festival, Cardiff and district

22 June
North Wales Motor Show, Eirias Park, Colwyn Bay

28 June
Ceiriog Valley Country Show, Chirk Castle

29 June
Heritage Festival, Merthyr Tydfil

4 - 6 July
Beyond the Border - The Welsh International Festival of Storytelling, St Donat's Castle, nr Llantwit Major. (provisional)

Morris in the Forest Festival (Morris dancing, forest walks, etc), Llanwrtyd Wells.

9th North Wales Bluegrass Festival, Conwy

12 July
Mid Wales Festival of Transport, Powis Castle, Welshpool

14 - 26 July
Gower Music Festival

17 - 26
Welsh Proms, St David's Hall, Cardiff

23 - 30 July
Ian Rush International Soccer Tournament (youth soccer), Aberystwyth

2 August
Brecon County Show

3 - 9 August
Conwy River Festival

7 - 10 August
Mountain Bike Festival, Llanwrtyd Wells

9 August
Chepstow Agricultural Show

Eglwysbach Show, nr Colwyn Bay

19 - 21
Pembrokeshire County Show, Withybush, nr Haverfordwest

20 August
Vale of Glamorgan Agricultural Show, Cowbridge

25 August
Caerleon Country Carnival

Merthyr Show, Merthyr Tydfil

World Bog-Snorkelling Championships, Llanwrtyd Wells

28 August
Monmouthshire Show, Monmouth

5 - 15 September (provisional)
Vale of Glamorgan Festival, Vale of Glamorgan and Cardiff

6 September
Llandysul Show

13 September
Usk Show

16 - 19 September
Welsh International Four Days of Walks, Llanwrtyd Wells

21 September
Leukaemia Research Fund Vintage Car Rally, Tredegar House and Park, Newport

27 October - 1 November
(provisional)
Holyhead Arts Festival

14 - 23 November
Mid Wales Beer Festival, Llanwrtyd Wells

2 December
Royal Welsh Agricultural Winter Fair, Builth Wells

History and Heritage

Wales's past is etched in its landscape. In your travels, you'll come across prehistoric and Roman remains, mighty medieval castles, manor houses and mansions, and a fascinating industrial heritage.

Carreg Samson, in the Preseli Hills near Newport

Ancient stones and medieval strongholds

Skeletal Pentre Ifan Cromlech in Pembrokeshire's Preseli Hills is one of many prehistoric monuments scattered throughout Wales. Thousands of years later, the Romans left camps, roadways, an extraordinary amphitheatre and bath-house at Caerleon and unique gold mine at Pumsaint. But more than anything else, Wales is famous for its castles – mighty medieval monuments such as Caernarfon, Conwy and Caerphilly, as well as dramatic ruins like Carreg Cennen, Llandeilo and remote Castell-y-Bere hidden beneath Cader Idris.

Historic houses

History also lives on at Llancaiach Fawr, a restored Tudor manor house in the Rhymney Valley which recreates the times of the Civil War. You can glimpse into grand country houses at National Trust properties such as Plas Newydd on Anglesey, Welshpool's Powis Castle and Erddig near Wrexham (an unusual 'upstairs, downstairs' house). Dignified Tredegar House at Newport is another mansion with two sides to its personality – a glittering interior together with preserved servants' quarters.

Industrial memories

In Wales, you'll discover gripping monuments to the era of coal, slate, iron and steel. 'King Coal's' reign is movingly remembered at places like the Big Pit Mining Museum, Blaenafon, and the Rhondda Heritage Park, Trehafod. North Wales's slate industry has a successful modern spin-off at the popular Llechwedd Slate Caverns, Blaenau Ffestiniog – and slate is again the theme at the Gloddfa Ganol Mine, also in Blaenau Ffestiniog, and Llanberis's Welsh Slate Museum.

Makers of Wales | At Your Service

Welcome Host

Customer care is our top priority. It's what our Welcome Host scheme is all about. Open to everyone from hotel staff to taxi drivers, the scheme places the emphasis on hospitality and first-class service. Welcome Host badge or certificate holders are part of a tradition of friendliness. Look out for the symbol on the following pages – it's a welcoming sign.

Makers of Wales, the Millennium Festival Campaign for Wales, is all about the people of Wales and how, over time, they have created a unique identity through the country's language, customs and built and natural heritage. The festival theme for 1997 is 'Myth, Legend and Faith'. Throughout the year there will be events and exhibitions staged by many organisations ranging from local community groups to Cadw-Welsh Historic Monuments, the Countryside Council for Wales, the National Museums and Galleries of Wales and the National Trust. Look out for the distinctive Makers of Wales symbol on your travels.

A Taste of Wales

A Taste of Wales-Blas ar Gymru is a scheme created to encourage and promote Wales's distinctive culinary identity. Taste of Wales members include hotels, restaurants, bistros, tea rooms and inns. The food they serve ranges from established favourites to creative modern dishes, reflecting the Taste of Wales philosophy of using local ingredients when preparing traditional and innovative Welsh recipes. Wales is fortunate to have such an abundant larder of fresh local produce, including superb seafoods, top-quality Welsh lamb and wonderful cheeses.

St David's Cathedral

Further details from:
Campaign Co-ordinator, Makers of Wales,
4th Floor, Empire House, Cardiff CF1 6DN
Tel: (01222) 471121

So Accessible

One of Wales's big advantages is its ease of access. It's only a few hours by road and rail from most of the UK's main centres. Travel to Wales doesn't take up much time or money, so you can enjoy your holiday or short break to the full. And when you arrive, you'll be back in the days when driving was a pleasure on traffic-free highways and byways.

By car

Travel to South and West Wales is easy on the M4 and onward dual carriageway systems.

With the opening of the Second Severn Crossing, traffic for Cardiff and West Wales follows the revised route of the M4 across the new bridge. For Chepstow and the Wye Valley you'll need the M48 (the old route of the M4) across the original bridge. The A55 North Wales coast 'Expressway' whisks traffic past the old bottlenecks, including Conwy. Mid Wales is easily reached by the M54 which links with the M6/M5/M1. Driving around Wales is a delight, for most highways remain blissfully quiet and uncrowded apart from a few peak summer weekends. Wales is a small yet scenically varied country, so there's no need to rush - take your time and enjoy it to the full.

By rail

Fast and frequent Great Western InterCity services run between London Paddington and Cardiff (via Reading and Swindon), taking only 2 hours. This hourly service (every half hour at peak times) also runs to Newport, Bridgend, Port Talbot, Neath and Swansea, with onward connections to West Wales. Fast InterCity trains also link London (Euston) with the North Wales coast, serving both Bangor and Holyhead, and the North East of England to South Wales.

In addition, Regional Railways operates a direct Alphaline service from London Waterloo (via Woking and Basingstoke) to Cardiff and other main stations in South and West Wales. Regional Railways also runs other services into Wales. There are also convenient and comfortable Alphaline trains to Cardiff (and other destinations in South and West Wales) from:

- Manchester/the North West
- Brighton/Portsmouth/Salisbury/ Southampton
- The West of England/Bristol
- Nottingham/Birmingham/ Gloucester.

For Mid Wales there are Alphaline trains to Aberystwyth and other Mid Wales resorts from Birmingham via Shrewsbury. This service connects with InterCity trains from London Euston at Birmingham.

A 'North West Express' service operates from Manchester to the North Wales coast and Holyhead via Crewe and Chester.There are also trains from the West Midlands to North Wales.

Exploring Wales by train is a delight. Scenic routes include the beautiful Heart of Wales line from Shrewsbury to Swansea, the Conwy Valley line from Llandudno Junction to Blaenau Ffestiniog, and the Cambrian Coast line, which runs along the mountain-backed shoreline from Pwllheli to Machynlleth and Aberystwyth.

Ask about the money-saving unlimited-travel Rover and Ranger fares, some of which include the use of bus services.

By coach

National Express provides a nationwide network of express coach services, many of which have been upgraded to Rapide specification with on-board washrooms and light refreshments available. Convenient services to Wales operate from London's Victoria Coach Station and from almost all other major towns and cities in England and Scotland.

Towns and resorts throughout Wales are, of course, connected by a whole range of local and regional services. Details from Tourist Information Centres and local bus stations. You can travel cross-country by the TrawsCambria service running between Cardiff and Bangor (via Aberystwyth). Within North and Mid Wales you can combine coach and rail services through unlimited-travel Rover and Ranger tickets (see 'By rail' for details).

Further information

Please see 'Further Information' at the back of this guide for rail and coach travel information offices, plus details of sea and air services to Wales.

MILEAGE CHART

	MILES	JOURNEY TIME BY CAR
Birmingham – Aberystwyth	125	2 hrs 49 mins
Canterbury – Cardiff	219	3 hrs 56 mins
Coventry – Barmouth	133	2 hrs 51 mins
Exeter – Swansea	161	2 hrs 25 mins
Leeds – Llandudno	131	2 hrs 3 mins
London – Cardiff	155	2 hrs 40 mins
London – Tenby	245	4 hrs 7 mins
Manchester – Caernarfon	110	1 hr 58 mins
Nottingham – Swansea	202	3 hrs 10 mins
Peterborough – Aberystwyth	208	4 hrs 30 mins
Newcastle-upon-Tyne – Llandudno	230	3 hrs 56 mins
Reading – Carmarthen	177	2 hrs 40 mins
York – Welshpool	155	2 hrs 55 mins

Where to Stay

The remainder of this guide is filled with a great choice of places to stay – everything from comfortable resort and country house hotels to friendly farmhouses, good-value guest houses to fully equipped city hotels ideal for a business stopover. You can choose in confidence, because the accommodation featured – from the remotest farmhouse to the largest hotel – has been thoroughly checked out by a visit from one of WTB's approved inspectors. Not only that, but we also spell out clearly the quality and standards for you.

Making the grade

Look out first for the GRADES – they're your guide to QUALITY.

APPROVED	– Good
COMMENDED	– Very Good
HIGHLY COMMENDED	– Excellent
DE LUXE	– A special accolade representing exceptional comfort and service

Focus on facilities

Then there are CROWNS, which tell you how WELL EQUIPPED the accommodation is. The more facilities, the higher the Crown rating. The range runs from Welcome Home 🏠 (clean and comfortable accommodation) to Five Crowns ♛♛ (an extensive range of facilities and services).

Award Winners

If you want extra-special guest house or farmhouse accommodation, look out for the places which have won the coveted Wales Tourist Board Award All Award winners will have the Highly Commended or De Luxe grade, and proprietors will have successfully completed a tourism training course covering most aspects of running an accommodation enterprise.

Cyclists and Walkers Welcome

 Cycling and walking enthusiasts should look out for the 'bike' and 'boot' symbols in the following advertising section (some properties qualify for both symbols, others just the one). They are displayed by places which have undertaken to provide features which cyclists and/or walkers always find welcome. These include drying facilities for wet clothes and boots, secure lockable areas for bikes, availability of packed lunches and so on. You'll even be greeted with a welcoming cup of tea or coffee on arrival!

Accommodating wheelchair users

The Wales Tourist board actively encourages the provision of facilities for disabled visitors. Properties are visited on request to assess their suitability.

 Accessible to a wheelchair user travelling independently

 Accessible to a wheelchair user travelling with assistance

 Accessible to a wheelchair user able to walk a few paces and up a maximum of three steps

For further details, please see 'Information for visitors with disabilities' in the 'Further Information/ Useful Addresses' section of this guide.

Llyn Gwynant, Snowdonia

Making Your Booking

Book direct

Telephone or write to the place of your choice direct. It's as simple as that. If you phone, please check the prices and follow up the call with a letter of confirmation enclosing whatever deposit you've agreed with the proprietor.

Book through a TIC

Look out for this symbol on the following pages. It means that you can book the featured accommodation through any networked Tourist Information Centre.

Or Book by Freephone

You can book any accommodation through the following freephone numbers:

North Wales	(0800) 834820
Mid Wales	(0800) 273747
South and West Wales	(0800) 243731

Prices

Please note that all prices are PER PERSON, based on TWO PEOPLE sharing a double or twin room. SINGLE OCCUPANCY will usually be charged extra, and there may be supplements for private bath/shower. Daily rates are for bed and breakfast. Weekly rates are for dinner, B&B.

All prices quoted include VAT at the current rate (17$^1/_2$%). Prices and other specific holiday information in this guide were supplied to the Wales Tourist Board during July-October 1996. So do check all prices and facilities before confirming your booking.

Children stay free

Many hotels, guest houses and farmhouses offer free accommodation for children if sharing their parents' room (you only pay for their meals). It's always worth asking about reductions, for most operators will offer child discounts. Family holiday hotels, especially in major resorts, also cater for one-parent families.

16

Deposits

Most operators will ask for a deposit when a reservation is being made. Some establishments may request payment in advance of arrival.

Cancellation and insurance

When you confirm a holiday booking, please bear in mind that you are entering a legally binding contract which entitles the proprietor to compensation if you fail to take up the accommodation. It's always wise to arrange holiday insurance to cover you for cancellation and other unforeseen eventualities. If you have to alter your travel plans, please advise the holiday operator or proprietor immediately.

Any problems?

We care about our visitors' views and encourage you to make any comments you may have about your stay to the proprietor of the establishment at the time of your visit. In this way it may be possible to make your stay even more pleasurable and to arrange for new facilities and services to be provided in the future.

If you need to get in touch with the Wales Tourist Board about any aspect of your stay please contact the Visitor Services Dept, Wales Tourist Board, Brunel House, 2 Fitzalan Road, Cardiff CF2 1 UY (Tel. 01222 475281/475278). We will let you have a reply to your letter or call within 15 working days of its receipt.

Lower Fishguard

Key to Symbols

H	Hotel
GH	Guest House
FH	Farmhouse
FGH	Farm Guest House
🛏	Total number of bedrooms
🛏	Number of en-suite bedrooms
AWARD	Recipient of the Wales Tourist Board Guest House/Farmhouse Award
🏅	Welcome Host (minimum of 50% of staff trained)
🏅 GOLD	Welcome Host Gold Award (minimum of 90% of staff trained).
🚲	Facilities available for cyclists and/or walkers
P	Private car parking/garage facilities at establishment
🐕	Dogs/pets accepted into establishment by arrangement
C	Children under 12 accommodated free if sharing parents' room (meals charged extra)
🍷	Liquor licence
🔥	Central heating throughout
🚭	Areas provided for non-smokers
🚭	Totally non-smoking establishment
🍽	Evening meals available by prior arrangement
🌙	Special weekend/midweek or short break holidays available including Christmas or New Year
i	Accommodation may be booked through Networked Tourist Information Centres

Please note: The symbols, together with the descriptive wording in the following accommodation advertisements, have been provided by the proprietors.

Using This Guide

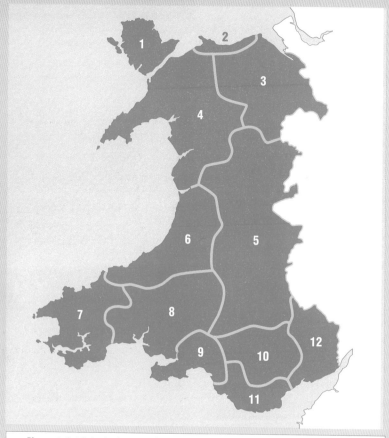

Please note that the borders between each area are only approximate. Places on or close to the border may choose to be listed under the area or areas of their choice.

It's easy to find your way around this guide. The rest of the book is filled with 'where to stay' information presented as follows. Firstly, we divide the accommodation up into Wales's 12 holiday areas (see the map and index below).

Then within each individual area, the resorts, towns and villages are listed alphabetically. Each place has a map reference enabling you to pinpoint it on the detailed gridded maps at the back of the book.

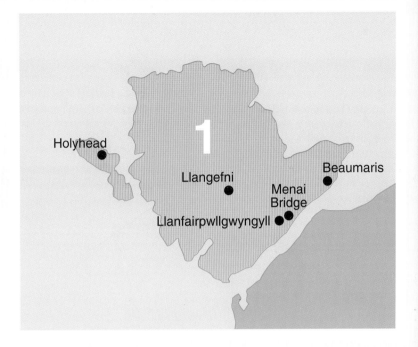

This island is a place of great natural beauty, history and heritage. The coastline is astonishingly varied – from the dunes of Newborough to the sea-cliffs of Holyhead Mountain and the open sands of Red Wharf Bay. Anglesey, with its small, stylish resorts, is the perfect destination for the quieter seaside holiday.

If you can drag yourself away from the beach you'll find a huge range of places to visit – ancient burial chambers, the mansion of Plas Newydd, Beaumaris Castle and the award-winning Anglesey Sea Zoo to name but a few. If you're a birdwatcher, bring your binoculars to the cliffs at South Stack or the sands at Malltraeth. For sailors, there are the sheltered waters of the Menai Strait between Anglesey and the mainland of North Wales.

It's a fact...

Opened in 1826, Thomas Telford's elegant Menai Suspension Bridge was the world's first large iron suspension bridge. In the 19th century the puffin inhabitants of Puffin Island off the Anglesey coast were caught, filleted, pickled in brine and served as a delicacy! Llanddwyn island is dedicated to 'Dwynwen the Pure', the patron saint of Welsh lovers. The world-famous town with the longest name is Llanfairpwllgwyngyllgogerychwyrndrobwllllantysiliogogogoch, which means 'St Mary's (Church) by the white aspen over the whirlpool, and St Tysilio's (Church) by the red cave'.

Ae3   Beaumaris

Beautifully sited Anglesey coastal resort with splendid 13th-century castle. Other historic buildings along main street, Victorian Gaol, enchanting Museum of Childhood, fascinating old courthouse, and Beaumaris Marine World. Yachting centre with golf course and excellent fishing. Sixteenth-century Penmon Priory nearby. Ideal touring centre for Snowdonia with superb views of mountains across Menai Strait.

Ad2   Brynteg

Village near east coast of Anglesey and a number of beautiful beaches. The attractive resort of Benllech and vast sands of Red Wharf Bay are close by.

Ac1   Cemaes

Quaint unspoilt village with stone quay on rugged northern shores of Anglesey. Boating, fishing and swimming. Wylfa Nuclear Power Station open to the public.

Ac2   Llannerch-y-medd

Central Anglesey village with easy access to island's beaches. Visit Din Llugwy, ancient remains of fortified village, the working windmill at Llanddeusant and the Llyn Alaw Visitor Centre.

Beaumaris

H | Bishopsgate House Hotel

Castle Street,
Beaumaris LL58 8BB
Tel: (01248) 810302
Fax: (01248) 810166

HIGHLY COMMENDED

Relax and enjoy comfortable en-suite accommodation, delicious freshly prepared food, fine wines and a warm welcome at our elegant georgian townhouse hotel. Conveniently situated close to the centre of the historic castle town of Beaumaris, just metres from the shores of the Menai Strait. Excellent value short breaks available throughout the year. *i*

		NIGHTLY B & B PER PERSON		WEEKLY D, B & B PER PERSON		🛏 9 🛁 9
		MIN £	MAX £	MIN £	MAX £	OPEN
		26.00	30.00	245.00	270.00	2 - 12

GH | Tyn Pistyll

Beach Road, Llanddona,
Beaumaris LL58 8UN
Tel: (01248) 811224
Fax: (01248) 811224

HIGHLY COMMENDED

A quiet country house with a relaxing friendly atmosphere. Stunning views over Red Wharf Bay. Unspoilt Llanddona Beach is $1/2$ mile away. Beaumaris 4 miles away where there are many nice bistros to sample. En-suite rooms with high quality facilities. Large Welsh breakfast served or special diets catered for. Many outdoor attractions in the vicinity. Horse riding, sailing, go kart racing, walking or just relax and enjoy the views. *i*

		NIGHTLY B & B PER PERSON		WEEKLY D, B & B PER PERSON		🛏 4 🛁 3
		MIN £	MAX £	MIN £	MAX £	OPEN
		20.00	25.00	-	-	2 - 10

GH | Treddolphin Guest House

Beach Road,
Cemaes LL67 0ET
Tel: (01407) 710388

COMMENDED

Situated in an elevated position overlooking bay and coast. Presenting good home cooking. All bedrooms have private shower and H&C. There is free babysitting and courtesy tea and biscuits in lounge in the evening. Ideal for relaxing holiday. Abundant unspoilt coastal scenery and beaches. Near 18 hole golf course. Ample parking. Village minutes walk away. Competitive rates. Children half price up to 16 years old sharing parents' room. For a welcoming service ring Roberta and Harold Williams. *i*

		NIGHTLY B & B PER PERSON		WEEKLY D, B & B PER PERSON		🛏 8 🛁
		MIN £	MAX £	MIN £	MAX £	OPEN
		13.00	13.50	105.00	105.00	1 - 12

H | Henllys Hall Hotel & Golf Course

Beaumaris LL58 8HU
Tel: (01248) 810412
Fax: (01248) 811511

COMMENDED

Set within 125 acres of mature park land overlooking the Menai Strait and beyond, this magnificent country house hotel is the ideal retreat. Our facilities include an extensive leisure club, 18 hole golf course in the grounds and woodland walks.
Our Hampton Room Restaurant prides itself on only using local produce, and our Head Chef, Nick Davies is a member of the Welsh Olympic Culinary Squad. *i*

		NIGHTLY B & B PER PERSON		WEEKLY D, B & B PER PERSON		🛏 23 🛁 23
		MIN £	MAX £	MIN £	MAX £	OPEN
		30.00	50.00	315.00	385.00	1 - 12

H | California Hotel & Restaurant

Brynteg LL78 8JQ
Tel: (01248) 852360
Fax: (01248) 853547

HIGHLY COMMENDED

One of Anglesey's oldest and best known country taverns situated just 5 mins. from the seaside, village of Benllech and 30 mins. from Holyhead, Irish Ferries and the Snowdonia Mountains. Now extensively refurbished, this family run hotel offers the best of old and new. Excellent restaurant and wine list, with bar food also available. All the bedrooms are en-suite and fully equipped. Large private car park. Golfing nearby. Colour brochure available on request. *i*

		NIGHTLY B & B PER PERSON		WEEKLY D, B & B PER PERSON		🛏 5 🛁 5
		MIN £	MAX £	MIN £	MAX £	OPEN
		22.00	-	154.00	-	1 - 12

FH | Drws y Coed

Llannerch-y-medd
LL71 8AD
Tel: (01248) 470473

HIGHLY COMMENDED

AWARD

With wonderful panoramic views of Snowdonia, this beautifully appointed farmhouse on a 550 acre working farm, is situated in peaceful wooded countryside. Centrally situated to explore Anglesey. Comfortable en-suite bedrooms are tastefully decorated with all facilities. Central heating. Inviting spacious lounge with log fire. Delicious meals. Games room. Historic farmstead. Lovely private walks. Farm Holiday Guide Diploma Award. Visitors return year after year to enjoy the warm hospitality from Mrs Jane Bown. *i*

		NIGHTLY B & B PER PERSON		WEEKLY D, B & B PER PERSON		🛏 3 🛁 3
		MIN £	MAX £	MIN £	MAX £	OPEN
		20.00	22.50	215.00	215.00	1 - 12

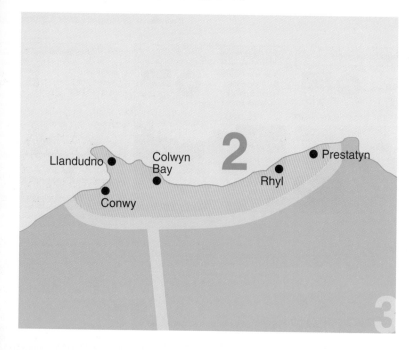

North Wales's sandy coastal strip is famous for its popular mixture of big beaches, colourful attractions and family entertainment. But within this formula there's scope for variety. Historic Conwy, with its ancient walls and castle, still retains a medieval air. Llandudno, the stately 'Queen' of the Welsh resorts, remains faithful to its Victorian roots while at the same time catering for the needs of today's visitors. For sheer seaside harmony, there's nothing quite like the view along its seafront from the headland above. Colwyn Bay, Rhyl and Prestatyn offer unpretentious fun and amusement, with huge beaches and an even larger choice of attractions, including the marvellous Welsh Mountain Zoo (Colwyn Bay), the Sun Centre (Rhyl) and the Nova Centre (Prestatyn).

It's a fact...

Llandudno's pier is over 900m/3000ft long. The resort's alpine-style Cabin Lift, one of the longest in Britain, carries passengers by cablecar for over a mile from the seafront to the summit of the Great Orme headland. Conwy has Britain's 'smallest house', a tiny fisherman's cottage on the quay. The Welsh Mountain Zoo at Colwyn Bay is owned by the Zoological Society of Wales, an educational and scientific charity. Rhyl's 73m-/240ft-high Skytower offers spectacular views from Snowdonia to Liverpool. Prestatyn is at one end of the 168-mile Offa's Dyke Path.

Bb4　　Conwy　

Historic town with mighty castle and complete ring of medieval town walls. Dramatic estuary setting. Many ancient buildings including Aberconwy House. Telford Suspension Bridge, popular fish quay, spectacular wall walks. Golf, pony trekking, Butterfly House, art gallery, aquarium, pleasure cruises. Tiny 'smallest house' on quay. Touring centre for Snowdonia.

Bb3　　Llandudno　

Premier coastal resort of North Wales with everything the holidaymaker needs. Two beaches, spacious promenade, Victorian pier, excellent shopping. Donkey rides. Punch and Judy, ski slope. Alice in Wonderland exhibition, art gallery, museum, old copper mines open to the public, splendid North Wales Theatre. Visit the Great Orme headland above the resort and ride by cabinlift or tramway. Conference centre. Many daily excursions.

andudno

Conwy Llandudno

H | Sychnant Pass Hotel

Sychnant Pass Road,
Conwy LL32 8BJ
Tel: (01492) 596868
Fax: (01492) 596868

COMMENDED

The hotel is a unique country house in a tranquil setting on the edge of the Snowdonia National Park. With en-suite comfort, cosy lounge, superb food and fine wines - Welsh dishes and wines a speciality. The new owners offer their guests total commitment and a caring service, thus promoting an ambience to delight the discerning. Other amenities include a drying facility for outdoor clothing and an all day coffee lounge.

		NIGHTLY B & B PER PERSON		WEEKLY D, B & B PER PERSON		🛏 10
P 🍴	🛁 🎨					🛁 10
		MIN £ 25.00	MAX £ 30.00	MIN £ 156.00	MAX £ 180.00	OPEN 2 - 12

H | Hafod-y-Mor Hotel

Hill Terrace,
Llandudno
LL30 2LS
Tel: (01492) 876925
Fax: (01492) 860527

AWAITING GRADING

Ideally situated with magnificent views. Convenient for Great Orme, Cable car, tram, ski-slope, Happy Valley, pier and shops. All rooms en-suite with colour TV, tea and coffee, clock radio and hairdryer. Beautiful food, spotlessly clean, patio. Residents' bar. Professionally run by the same family for the last nine years.

		NIGHTLY B & B PER PERSON		WEEKLY D, B & B PER PERSON		🛏 10
P 🍴	🛁 🎨					🛁 10
	🍴	MIN £ 20.00	MAX £ 26.00	MIN £ 210.00	MAX £ 252.00	OPEN 3 - 10

H | Pier Gardens Hotel

North Parade,
Llandudno LL30 2LP
Tel: (01492) 877114

Seafront hotel near pier and shops. All bedrooms with private bathroom, colour television, radio, tea/coffee maker, hairdryer. Ironing facilities, central heating. Five course evening dinner served daily, choice of menu. Car park at rear. Please phone or write for brochure.

		NIGHTLY B & B PER PERSON		WEEKLY D, B & B PER PERSON		🛏 12
P 🍴	🛁 🎨					🛁 12
	🍴	MIN £ 20.00	MAX £ 20.00	MIN £ 161.00	MAX £ 161.00	OPEN 3 - 10

H | Epperstone Hotel

15 Abbey Road,
Llandudno LL30 2EE
Tel: (01492) 878746
Fax: (01492) 871223

DE LUXE

GOLD

Edwardian Elegance. Beautifully appointed detached hotel in award winning gardens. Spacious well appointed rooms with all facilities and fully en-suite. Ground floor twin bedroom for those with less mobility. Victorian conservatory, elegant lounge, gives peace and tranquillity. Chef prepared menus. Car park. Outstanding service, with great value guaranteed.

		NIGHTLY B & B PER PERSON		WEEKLY D, B & B PER PERSON		🛏 8
P 🍴	🐾 🚭					🛁 8
🛁 🎨	🍴	MIN £ 25.00	MAX £ 28.00	MIN £ 220.00	MAX £ 240.00	OPEN 1 - 12

H | Lynton House Hotel

80 Church Walks,
Llandudno LL30 2HD
Tel: (01492) 875057/875009

HIGHLY COMMENDED

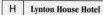

A homely hotel close to promenade, pier, skiing, shops and all amenities. All rooms decorated to a high standard with en-suite bathroom, colour TV, tea/coffee tray and telephone. Highly recommended home cooking with choice of menu. Vegetarian and special diets catered for. Four poster rooms. Parking.

		NIGHTLY B & B PER PERSON		WEEKLY D, B & B PER PERSON		🛏 13
P C	🐾					🛁 13
🚭 🎨	🍴	MIN £ 20.00	MAX £ 21.00	MIN £ 195.00	MAX £ 205.00	OPEN 1 - 12

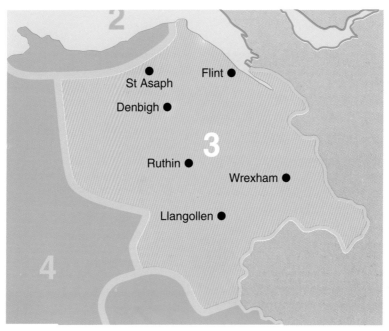

Wales's border country is a mix of rolling green hills, lovely valleys, high moor and forest. The airy Clwydian Range guards the broad and fertile Vale of Clwyd – one of Wales's richest farming areas – which is dotted with historic towns. The valley around Llangollen is much deeper, its steep-sided hills rising to dramatic heights with names like 'World's End'. The wild moorlands above Denbigh are covered in heather and forest – and the waters of Llyn Brenig, a huge reservoir with many leisure facilities. There's much to see and do in this exhilarating area – walking, riding, canal cruising, and visiting places like Bodelwyddan Castle, where paintings from the National Portrait Gallery are exhibited, and Erddig, Wrexham, an unusual 'upstairs, downstairs' country house owned by the National Trust.

It's a fact…

The North Wales Borderlands is home to six of the seven 'Wonders of Wales' - Pistyll Rhaeadr Falls, Wrexham Steeple, Overton Yew Trees, Llangollen Bridge and Gresford's Bells. St Winefride's Well, the sixth 'wonder', is visited to this day by pilgrims who come to bathe in its legendary waters. Beatrix Potter found inspiration for her Flopsy Bunnies illustrations at Gwaynynog near Denbigh. Gladstone's birth at Hawarden is commemorated by his statue and by the world-famous St Deiniol's Library which he founded.

Be7   Corwen

Pleasant market town in Vale of Edeyrnion. Livestock market held regularly. Fishing in River Dee, swimming pool, good walks. Well-located touring centre for Snowdonia and border country.

Be5   Denbigh

Castled town in Vale of Clwyd with much historic interest. Friary and museum. Pony trekking, riding, fishing, golf, tennis and bowls. Indoor heated swimming pool. Centrally located for enjoying the rolling hills of North-east Wales, a rich farming area full of attractive villages.

Cb4   Holywell

Place of pilgrimage for centuries, the 'Lourdes of Wales' with St Winefride s Holy Well. Remains of Basingwerk Abbey (1131) nearby. Leisure centre with swimming pools. Interesting and attractive Greenfield Valley Heritage Park.

Llangollen

Ec1   Llangollen

Romantic town on River Dee, famous for its International Musical Eisteddfod; singers and dancers from all over the world come here every July. The town's many attractions include a canal museum, pottery, weavers, ECTARC European Centre for Traditional and Regional Cultures and a standard-gauge steam railway. Plas Newydd (home of 'Ladies of Llangollen' fame) is nearby. Valle Crucis Abbey is 2 miles away in a superb setting and ruined Castell Dinas Brân overlooks the town. Browse through the town's little shops; stand on its 14th-century stone bridge; cruise along the canal. Golf course and wonderful walking in surrounding countryside.

Be4   St Asaph

Tiny city with the smallest cathedral in Britain, scene of the annual North Wales Music Festival. Prehistoric Cefn Caves nearby. Pleasantly situated on River Elwy in verdant Vale of Clwyd. Three important historic sites on doorstep – medieval Rhuddlan Castle, Bodelwyddan Castle (with noted art collection) and Bodrhyddan Hall.

H	Central Hotel

The Square,
Holyhead Road,
Corwen LL21 0DE
Tel: (01490) 412462

For all year round holidays and short breaks. A warm welcome and excellent cuisine await you. Situated at the foot of the Berwyn Mountains on a bend of the beautiful River Dee, it is the perfect centre for walking, sightseeing, a gateway to the "wilds of North Wales" and central to Llangollen, Ruthin and Bala.

		NIGHTLY B & B PER PERSON		WEEKLY D, B & B PER PERSON		🛏 10
						🍴 10
		MIN £	MAX £	MIN £	MAX £	OPEN
		39.00	45.00	192.50	215.00	1 - 12

GH	Cayo Guest House

74 Vale Street,
Denbigh LL16 3BW
Tel: (01745) 812686

COMMENDED

Long established centrally situated guest house. Ideal for touring North Wales. Excellent area for walking, golf, gliding, cycling, angling. Good food using local produce. Special menus on request. Well behaved dogs and children welcome!. AA QQ. Pick up service for "Offa's Dykers"

		NIGHTLY B & B PER PERSON		WEEKLY D, B & B PER PERSON		🛏 6
						🍴 4
		MIN £	MAX £	MIN £	MAX £	OPEN
		17.00	17.00	238.00	238.00	1 - 12

FH	Greenhill Farm

Bryn Celyn,
Holywell CH8 7QF
Tel: (01352) 713270

COMMENDED

Our 16th century farmhouse affords beautiful views across the Dee Estuary to the Wirral Peninsula and beyond. Set in beautiful gardens, which include a children's play area. The oak beamed house includes bedroom with an inglenook and an oak panelled dining room. All rooms include TV and tea facilities with 2 en-suite. Guests are offered a warm welcome and fresh, locally produced foods. Children are especially welcome on the farm.

		NIGHTLY B & B PER PERSON		WEEKLY D, B & B PER PERSON		🛏 4
						🍴 2
		MIN £	MAX £	MIN £	MAX £	OPEN
		16.50	-	-	-	3 - 10

H	Abbey Grange Hotel

Horseshoe Pass Road,
Llangollen LL20 8DD
Tel: (01978) 860753
Fax: (01978) 869070

COMMENDED

Just 1½ miles from the charming country town of Llangollen. All rooms are en-suite with tea/coffee facilities and TV. Full central heating. Magnificent views to all sides. Large car park. Children welcome. Food available all day. Friendly staff.

		NIGHTLY B & B PER PERSON		WEEKLY D, B & B PER PERSON		🛏 8
						🍴 8
		MIN £	MAX £	MIN £	MAX £	OPEN
		21.00	23.00	189.00	203.00	1 - 12

Llantysilio Mountain, near Llangollen

Llangollen St Asaph

H	Golden Pheasant Hotel

Glyn Ceiriog,
Nr. Llangollen LL20 7BB
Tel: (01691) 718281
Fax: (01691) 718479

Relaxing atmosphere, good food and friendly staff make this 18th century hotel the ideal base for exploring the unspoilt valleys of Llangollen. Easy to reach - only 15 minutes A5. Well stocked bar. Restaurant and snack room with picturesque views over garden. Whirlpool baths, four poster beds. Special golfing packages.

		NIGHTLY B & B PER PERSON		WEEKLY D, B & B PER PERSON			19
							19
		MIN £	MAX £	MIN £	MAX £	OPEN	
		27.50	37.50	250.00	300.00	1 - 12	

FGH	Tyn Celyn Farmhouse

Tyndwr,
Llangollen LL20 8AR
Tel: (01978) 861117

Spacious oak beamed farmhouse on the outskirts of Llangollen situated in a peaceful valley with beautiful views. All bedrooms have en-suite bathrooms, beverage tray, telelvision and central heating. Ideally situated for all local amenities and for visiting Snowdonia and Chester. Just 1 1/2 miles from town centre. Ample secure parking.

		NIGHTLY B & B PER PERSON		WEEKLY D, B & B PER PERSON			3
							3
		MIN £	MAX £	MIN £	MAX £	OPEN	
		18.00	20.00	-	-	1 - 12	

FGH	Plas Penucha

Caerwys,
Mold CH7 5BH
Tel: (01352) 720210

Welcome to this 16th century farmhouse altered over succeeding generations but retaining sense of history and serenity in comfortable surroundings. Extensive gardens overlooking Clwydian hills. Spacious lounge with extensive library and grand piano. Four well equipped bedrooms (2 en-suite). Full central heating and log fires. Two miles A55 Expressway. Ideal touring centre for North Wales coast, Snowdonia, Vale of Clwyd and Chester. Brochure from Nest Price.

		NIGHTLY B & B PER PERSON		WEEKLY D, B & B PER PERSON			4
							2
		MIN £	MAX £	MIN £	MAX £	OPEN	
		17.50	18.00	150.00	173.00	1 - 12	

Rhuddlan Castle

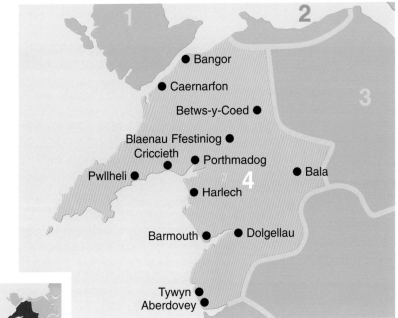

This part of Wales takes its name from the jagged pinnacle of Snowdon. Yet the Snowdonia National Park extends southwards for hundreds of square miles from Snowdon itself, all the way to Dolgellau and beyond, and eastwards to Bala. All of Wales's high and mighty mountains are here – Tryfan, the Glyders, the Carneddau, the Aran and Arennigs, and Cader Idris. Snowdonia, a place of surprising scenic variety, also has its oakwood vales, its forested hills, its lakes and rivers, its brooding moorlands. Mountains sweep down to the sea along a beautiful coastline of sandy beaches and estuaries. And along the Llŷn Peninsula – 'Snowdonia's arm' – you'll find some of the wildest coastal scenery in Britain as well as sheltered beaches and picturesque little resorts.

It's a fact...

The Snowdonia National Park covers 838 square miles. It was Wales's first national park, designated in 1951. Snowdonia's Welsh name is _Eryri_, which means 'the mountain of the eagles'. The peak of Snowdon stands at 1085m/3560ft, the highest mountain in England and Wales. The Llŷn Peninsula has the highest percentage of Welsh speakers in Wales (75%). Llŷn was declared an 'Area of Outstanding Natural Beauty' in 1956. Bwlch y Groes, the mountain road between Dinas Mawddwy and Bala, is Wales's highest road, climbing to 546m/1791ft. Bala Lake is Wales's largest natural lake.

Aa5 Aberdaron

Village on wild western shores of Llŷn, the 'Land's End of North Wales'. Attractive beach and spectacular headland with wonderful views across to Bardsey Island, the 'Isle of 20,000 Saints'. Dramatic coastal scenery all around. Porth-oer ('Whistling Sands') close by.

Db6 Aberdovey/Aberdyfi ⇌

Picturesque little resort and dinghy sailor's paradise on the Dovey Estuary. All watersports, thriving yacht club, good inns looking out over the bay and 18-hole golf links. Superb views towards hills and mountains.

De2 Bala

Traditional Welsh country town with tree-lined main street and interesting little shops. Narrow-gauge railway runs one side of Bala Lake, 4 miles long (the largest natural lake in Wales) and ringed with mountains. Golf, sailing, fishing, canoeing – a natural touring centre for Snowdonia.

Ae3 Bangor ⇌

Compact cathedral city of character overlooking the Menai Strait; gateway to Anglesey and Snowdonia's Ogwen Valley, with university college and 6th-century cathedral. Attractions include Theatr Gwynedd, Penrhyn Castle, museum and art gallery and an exquisitely renovated pier. Heated swimming pool, yachting and fishing.

Db4 Barmouth ⇌

Superbly located resort at the mouth of lovely Mawddach Estuary. Golden sands, miles of wonderful mountain and estuary walks nearby. Promenade, funfair, harbour and pony rides on the beach. Lifeboat and Shipwreck Centre museums. Good shops and inns. Excellent parking on seafront.

Ae6 Beddgelert

One of Snowdonia's loveliest mountain villages, home of the legend of Gelert, set amongst glorious scenery – Nant Gwynant Valley to the east and picturesque Aberglaslyn Pass to the south. Winner of numerous awards including 'Britain in Bloom'. Marvellous walks; Wordsworth made a famous dawn ascent of Snowdon from here. Ideal destination for that mountain break. Visit Sygun Copper Mine, a nearby attraction.

Bb6 Betws-y-Coed ⇌

Wooded village and popular mountain resort in picturesque setting where three rivers meet. Good touring centre, close to best mountain area of Snowdonia. Tumbling rivers and waterfalls emerge from a tangle of treetops. Trout fishing, craft shops, golf course, railway and motor museums, Snowdonia National Park Visitor Centre. Nature trails very popular with hikers. Swallow Falls a 'must'.

Ba7 Blaenau Ffestiniog ⇌

One-time centre of the Welsh slate industry, now attracts visitors who come to see two cavernous slate quarries – Llechwedd and Gloddfa Ganol – open to the public. Narrow-gauge Ffestiniog Railway runs from Porthmadog. Nearby Stwlan Dam, part of hydro-electric scheme, reached through marvellous mountain scenery. Visitor centre explains how electricity is generated.

Ad4 Caernarfon

Dominated by magnificent 13th-century castle, most famous of Wales's medieval fortresses. Many museums in castle, maritime museum in town. Caernarfon Air World at Dinas Dinlle, Segontium Roman Fort and Museum on hill above town. Popular sailing centre, old harbour, market square, Lloyd George statue. Holiday centre at gateway to Snowdonia. Parc Glynllifon nearby.

Bb4   Conwy

Historic town with mighty castle and complete ring of medieval town walls. Dramatic estuary setting. Many ancient buildings including Aberconwy House. Telford Suspension Bridge, popular fish quay, spectacular wall walks. Golf, pony trekking, Butterfly House, aquarium, pleasure cruises. Tiny 'smallest house' on quay. Touring centre for Snowdonia.

Ad7   Criccieth

Ideal family resort with good beach. Romantic ruined castle on headland overlooking sea. Salmon and trout in nearby rivers and lakes. Festival of Music and the Arts in June. Village of Llanystumdwy with Lloyd George Museum nearby.

Dd4   Dinas Mawddwy

Mountain village famed for its salmon and trout fishing and marvellous walks. On fringes of Snowdonia National Park. Visit the craft and tea shop at the old woollen mill. Drive over the spectacular Bwlch y Groes mountain road to Bala, the highest road in Wales.

Dc4   Dolgellau

Handsome stone-built market town which seems to have grown naturally out of the mountains. The heights of Cader Idris loom above the rooftops. Interesting shops, pubs, cafes. Museum of the Quakers in town centre. Visit a gold mine in nearby forest. Excellent base for touring the coast and countryside.

Db4   Fairbourne

Quiet resort with 2 miles of sand south of Mawddach Estuary. Railway buffs travel far to ride on its 1'3" gauge Fairbourne and Barmouth Steam Railway.

Da2   Harlech

Small, stone-built town dominated by remains of 13th-century castle – site of Owain Glyndŵr's last stand. Dramatically set on a high crag, the castle commands a magnificent panorama of rolling sand dunes, sea and mountains. Home of the 18-hole Royal St David's Golf Club. Shell Island nearby. Theatre and swimming pool. Visitors can explore the chambers of the Old Llanfair Slate Caverns just south of Harlech.

Da3   Llanbedr

Llanbedr and neighbouring Pensarn form a duo of attractive villages on the Ardudwy coast near Harlech. Maes Artro Village a popular family tourist attraction. Close to Shell Island at Mochras, and slate caverns. The wild Rhinog Mountains in the background are excellent for walking. Explore them from lovely Llyn Cwm Bychan.

Ae4   Llanberis

Popular centre for walkers and climbers, least difficult (5 miles) walk to Snowdon summit starts here. For easy ride up take Snowdon Mountain Railway. Many things to see and do in this lively mountain town – Llanberis Lake Railway, slate industry museum, unforgettable trip into the awesome tunnels of the Dinorwig Hydro-Electric Scheme, activity-packed Padarn Country Park, ancient Dolbadarn Castle, Bryn Brâs Castle at nearby Llanrug.

Dc5 Machynlleth ⇌

Historic market town near beautiful Dovey Estuary. Owain Glyndŵr's Parliament House in the wide handsome main street is now a museum and brass rubbing centre. Superbly equipped Bro Dyfi Leisure Centre offers wide range of activities. Celtica centre tells the story of Celtic myth and legend. Ancient and modern meet here; the inventive Centre for Alternative Technology is 3 miles away, just off the A487 to Dolgellau. Felin Crewi Flour Mill is off the A489 2 miles to the east.

Ae7 Porthmadog ⇌

Harbour town and shopping centre named after William Madocks, who built mile-long Cob embankment. Steam narrow-gauge Ffestiniog Railway runs to Blaenau Ffestiniog, with its slate caverns. Also Welsh Highland Railway. Pottery, maritime museum, car museum. Portmeirion Italianate village and good beaches nearby.

Ac7 Pwllheli ⇌

A small resort big in appeal to sailors; many craft are moored in its attractive marina. Promenade with excellent spacious beach, shopping, golf, leisure centre. River and sea fishing. Exciting Starcoast World, a major North Wales attraction, nearby.

Bb6 Trefriw

Woollen mill village on western side of Conwy Valley with Trefriw Wells Spa. Lakes at Llyn Geirionydd and Llyn Crafnant, both local beauty spots. Good walking country.

Da6 Tywyn ⇌

Seaside resort on Cardigan Bay, with beach activities, sea and river fishing and golf among its leading attractions. Good leisure centre. Narrow-gauge Talyllyn Railway runs inland from here and St Cadfan's Stone and Llanegryn Church are important Christian monuments. In the hills stands Castell-y-Bere, a native Welsh castle, and Bird Rock, a haven for birdlife.

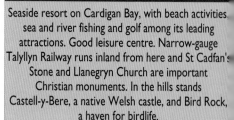

Centre For Alternative Technology, near Machynlleth

Porthmadog harbour, set against the mountains of Snowdonia

GH	Carreg Plas Guest House

Aberdaron,
Pwllheli LL53 8LH
Tel: (01758) 760308

17th century manor house of historic interest in secluded wooded grounds, two miles from Aberdaron, close to the Whistling Sands beach, surrounded by stretches of magnificent coastline largely National Trust owned. Range of room sizes, most having own facilities. Home cooking of high standard. Special reductions for children. Cots and high chairs provided. No smoking in the house.

		NIGHTLY B & B PER PERSON		WEEKLY D, B & B PER PERSON		🛏 6
						4
		MIN £	MAX £	MIN £	MAX £	OPEN
		17.50	24.50	180.00	230.00	1 - 12

H	Plas Penhelig Country House Hotel

Aberdovey LL35 0NA
Tel: (01654) 767676
Fax: (01654) 767783

HIGHLY COMMENDED

Plas Penhelig, a lovely country mansion enriched with oak panelling, set in beautifully landscaped gardens of particular interest to ornithologists, overlooking the lovely Dovey Estuary. Noted for good food, fine wines, personal attention. Relaxed atmosphere is a must for the discerning visitor. Ideally situated for exploring Snowdonia. Special breaks available. Advantageous terms for weekends and midweek breaks, including free golf, conference facilities.

		NIGHTLY B & B PER PERSON		WEEKLY D, B & B PER PERSON		🛏 11
						11
		MIN £	MAX £	MIN £	MAX £	OPEN
		40.00	45.50	364.00	392.00	3 - 12

GH	Frondderw Private Hotel

Stryd-y-Fron,
Bala LL23 7YD
Tel: (01678) 520301

COMMENDED

Period mansion quietly situated on the hillside overlooking Bala town and lake. All rooms have hot/cold, central heating, tea/coffee. Lounge, separate TV lounge. Ample free parking. Dinner optional. Vegetarians catered for. Ideal centre for sightseeing,walking, water sports, concessionary golf. Some rooms en-suite. Licensed. Home cooking.

		NIGHTLY B & B PER PERSON		WEEKLY D, B & B PER PERSON		🛏 8
						4
		MIN £	MAX £	MIN £	MAX £	OPEN
		15.00	21.00	161.00	203.00	3 - 11

H	Maybank Hotel & Restaurant

4 Penhelig Road,
Penhelig, Aberdovey LL35 0PT
Tel: (01654) 767500

HIGHLY COMMENDED

Family run, intimate and comfortable, Maybank enjoys the best sea/estuary views in Aberdovey. Recommended by leading Good Food Guides and complemented by an extensive and interesting wine list, dinner, B&B packages are excellent value for money. 6 bedrooms en-suite or with private bathroom. 26 seat restaurant and well stocked cosy bar. AA Rosettes 5 years in succession! Free parking in nearby car park. All food cooked to order. Special diets catered for. Same owners for 8 years.

		NIGHTLY B & B PER PERSON		WEEKLY D, B & B PER PERSON		🛏 6
						5
		MIN £	MAX £	MIN £	MAX £	OPEN
		23.95	29.95	259.00	280.00	2 - 11

H	Plas Coch Hotel

High Street,
Bala LL23 7AB
Tel: (01678) 520309
Fax: (01678) 521135

COMMENDED

*Situated in the centre of the lakeside town of Bala. Private car park. All bedrooms en-suite with colour TV, radio, telephone, tea/coffee facilities. Fully licensed restaurant with table d'hôte and à la carte menus. Come and enjoy good food and wine. "Taste of Wales" member. Concessionary golf at Bala Golf Club. Water sports holidays such as sailing, windsurfing and canoeing can be arranged nearby. A warm welcome awaits you from your resident host Dilwyn Morgan. AA/RAC**.*

		NIGHTLY B & B PER PERSON		WEEKLY D, B & B PER PERSON		🛏 10
						10
		MIN £	MAX £	MIN £	MAX £	OPEN
		32.50	32.50	252.00	252.00	1 - 12

FGH	Erw Feurig Farm Guest House

Cefnddwysarn,
Bala
LL23 7LL
Tel: (01678) 530262

HIGHLY COMMENDED

AWARD

A warm welcome awaits you at this pleasantly situated farm guest house. Spacious, comfortable bedrooms, with central heating and tea/coffee making facilities. Excellent breakfasts served in nice dining room. One ground floor room with private facilities. Two en-suite rooms. Fire certificate held. Private coarse fishing and snooker room available.

		NIGHTLY B & B PER PERSON		WEEKLY D, B & B PER PERSON		🛏 4
						3
		MIN £	MAX £	MIN £	MAX £	OPEN
		15.00	18.00	155.00	180.00	1 - 12

Bala Bangor Barmouth Beddgelert

FH	Bryn Melyn

Rhyduchaf,
Bala LL23 7SD
Tel: (01678) 520376

COMMENDED

Bryn Melyn situated 1½ miles from Bala. 5 Double rooms, 2 bathrooms. Comfortable sitting room. Home cooking. No smoking. A genuine Welsh welcome.

	NIGHTLY B & B PER PERSON		WEEKLY D, B & B PER PERSON		🛏 3
	MIN £	MAX £	MIN £	MAX £	OPEN
	14.00	16.00	152.00	154.00	1 - 12

H	Eryl Môr Hotel

2 Upper Garth Road,
Bangor LL57 2SR
Tel: (01248) 353789
Fax: (01248) 354042

HIGHLY COMMENDED

Twenty four bedroom, family run hotel, with splendid views of the unique Victorian pier, Menai Strait and Snowdonia. Restaurant and bar menus, good vegetarian and children's choice, fully licensed. En-suite rooms available. All rooms have TV, telephone, tea and coffee facilities. Sea view rooms can be reserved. Hotel and separate golf brochures available.

	NIGHTLY B & B PER PERSON		WEEKLY D, B & B PER PERSON		🛏 24
	MIN £	MAX £	MIN £	MAX £	OPEN
	16.75	22.50	-	-	1 - 12

FGH	Goetre Isaf Farmhouse

Caernarfon Road,
Bangor LL57 4DB
Tel: (01248) 364541
Fax: (01248) 364541

COMMENDED

Superb country situation with magnificent views. Although isolated, only 2 miles (3kms) from Bangor mainline station. Ideal touring centre. Imaginative farmhouse cooking. Vegetarians welcome. Special diets catered for. Ideal touring centre for the mountains of Snowdonia, Isle of Anglesey and the beaches of the Llŷn Peninsula. All bedrooms with dial phone facilities. Stabling by arrangement. Member of "Taste of Wales".

	NIGHTLY B & B PER PERSON		WEEKLY D, B & B PER PERSON		🛏 3
	MIN £	MAX £	MIN £	MAX £	OPEN
	13.50	18.50	136.50	189.00	1 - 12

FGH	Llwyndu Farmhouse & Restaurant

Llwyndu,
Llanaber,
Barmouth
LL42 1RR
Tel: (01341) 280144 Fax: (01341) 281236

HIGHLY COMMENDED
AWARD

Enjoy a relaxed and friendly stay in Peter and Paula Thompson's award winning 17th century farmhouse. Wonderful views over Cardigan Bay. Super rooms all of great individuality and very cosy. Here you can savour imaginative cuisine in a lovely atmosphere of oak beams, inglenooks, candlelight and music. For those who are seeking a beautiful, secluded spot where you really can relax in a truly laid back manner, then Llwyndu is just the place for you.

	NIGHTLY B & B PER PERSON		WEEKLY D, B & B PER PERSON		🛏 7
	MIN £	MAX £	MIN £	MAX £	OPEN
	25.00	29.00	255.00	275.00	1 - 12

H	Sygun Fawr Country House Hotel

Beddgelert LL55 4NE
Tel: (01766) 890258

HIGHLY COMMENDED

Secluded 17th century Welsh manor house standing in over 100 acres of its own land, commanding magnificent views of the Gwynant valley and Snowdon range. Ideal base for walking. En-suite rooms with tea/coffee facilities, Sauna available. Home cooking, vegetarian menu. Weekend and short breaks our speciality.

	NIGHTLY B & B PER PERSON		WEEKLY D, B & B PER PERSON		🛏 7
	MIN £	MAX £	MIN £	MAX £	OPEN
	26.50	26.50	264.00	264.00	2 - 10

H	Tanronnen Inn

Beddgelert LL55 4YB
Tel: (01766) 890347

HIGHLY COMMENDED

Situated at the head of the magnificent Glaslyn Pass in the heart of Snowdonia National Park. Fully refurbished to the highest standard with seven en-suite rooms available. Colour TV in bedrooms. Two intimate little bars. Access and Barclaycard accepted. Robinsons traditional draught beers.

	NIGHTLY B & B PER PERSON		WEEKLY D, B & B PER PERSON		🛏 7
	MIN £	MAX £	MIN £	MAX £	OPEN
	35.00	35.00	210.00	210.00	1 - 12

GH	Colwyn

Beddgelert LL55 4UY
Tel: (01766) 890.276

COMMENDED

Small cosy cottage guest house overlooking the river in the centre of a picturesque village at the foot of Snowdon. Spectacular scenery all round. Warm and friendly with an open stone hearth in a low-beamed lounge and small pretty bedrooms (most en-suite). Walkers muddy boots and pets welcome. B&B £17.50 - £19. 50. Booking advisable. (Low Season Breaks, Mon-Fri (4nts B&B) £60.00pp. Also tiny cottage sleeps two £165 weekly, S/C.

	NIGHTLY B & B PER PERSON		WEEKLY D, B & B PER PERSON		🛏 3
	MIN £	MAX £	MIN £	MAX £	OPEN
	18.00	-	-	-	1 - 12

Slide Sets

Ask about our attractive range of 35mm colour slides showing views of Wales, available at 75p per slide. For a complete list of subjects please contact the Photographic Librarian, Wales Tourist Board, Davis Street, Cardiff CF1 2FU (tel 01222-475215).

GH | Plas Colwyn Guest House

Beddgelert LL55 4UY
Tel: (01766) 890458

Enjoy a warm welcome, whilst exploring Snowdonia's beauty. Delicious fresh home cooked meals served in our intimate licensed restaurant. Special diets and vegetarians welcome. Guests' private lounge with log fire, and non-smoking throughout. Families, walkers and pets welcome. Private parking. All rooms with refreshment facilities. Some en-suite rooms. Co-ordinator for Northern Section of the Cambrian Way Walkers Association. *i*

P	C	NIGHTLY B & B PER PERSON		WEEKLY D, B & B PER PERSON		🛏 6
						🛁 3
		MIN £ 32.00	MAX £ 39.00	MIN £ -	MAX £ -	OPEN 1 - 12

H | Henllys Hotel (The Old Courthouse)

Old Church Road
Betws-y-Coed LL24 0AL
Tel: (01690) 710534
Fax: (01690) 710534

HIGHLY COMMENDED

Beautifully converted victorian magistrates court, set in peaceful riverside gardens. Spotless en-suite rooms with colour TV and tea/coffee makers. Superb food served in galleried dining room. Cosy fireside cocktail bar. Panoramic lounge overlooking Conwy river and valley. Private parking. Non smoking throughout. Warmest of welcomes. Residents and guests only. *i*

P	C	NIGHTLY B & B PER PERSON		WEEKLY D, B & B PER PERSON		🛏 10
						🛁 8
		MIN £ 23.00	MAX £ 27.00	MIN £ 255.00	MAX £ 270.00	OPEN 2 - 11

H | Ty Gwyn Hotel

Betws-y-Coed LL24 0SG
Tel: (01690) 710383 or 710787
Fax: (01690) 710383

HIGHLY COMMENDED

Award winning 16th century coaching inn, which has captured the charm and character of the period with oak beams, antique furniture and tasteful decor. All bedrooms are individually designed. Some with four poster beds. Excellent home cooking and an extensive wine list ensures a strong local following. *i*

P	C	🌳	NIGHTLY B & B PER PERSON		WEEKLY D, B & B PER PERSON		🛏 13
							🛁 9
			MIN £ 17.00	MAX £ 40.00	MIN £ 189.00	MAX £ 245.00	OPEN 1 - 12

H | Waterloo Hotel

Betws-y-Coed LL24 0AR
Tel: (01690) 710411
Fax: (01690) 710666

HIGHLY COMMENDED

The leading hotel in Snowdonia with hotel and motel rooms plus 4 self-catering cottages. Ideal location for touring Snowdonia and the beautiful coastline. All rooms en-suite with colour TV, telephone, tea/coffee tray, hairdryer, garden room, restaurant. Choice of bars, coffee shop.Indoor leisure and fitness complex.

P	🌳	NIGHTLY B & B PER PERSON		WEEKLY D, B & B PER PERSON		🛏 39
						🛁 39
		MIN £ 37.50	MAX £ 45.50	MIN £ 332.50	MAX £ 402.50	OPEN 1 - 12

GH | Aberconwy House

Llanwrst Road,
Betws-y-Coed LL24 0HD
Tel: (01690) 710202
Fax: (01690) 710800
E-mail: clive-muskus@celtic.co.uk

HIGHLY COMMENDED

Aberconwy House situated in a quiet position overlooking the popular and picturesque village. It is superbly and tastefully refurnished with all facilities for comfort and relaxation. There are beautiful views of the Llugwy Valley, surrounding mountains and the Conwy and Llugwy rivers. Robust breakfast and warm welcome awaiting from Ann and Clive Muskus. *i*

P	🌳	🚭	NIGHTLY B & B PER PERSON		WEEKLY D, B & B PER PERSON		🛏 8
							🛁 8
			MIN £ 22.00	MAX £ -	MIN £ -	MAX £ -	OPEN 1 - 12

GH | Bron Celyn Guest House

Llanwrst Road,
Betws-y-Coed
LL24 0HD.
Tel: (01690) 710333
Fax: (01690) 710111

HIGHLY COMMENDED

You will be assured of comfort and good home cooking at Bron Celyn. Situated overlooking the picturesque village of Betws-y-Coed. Easy access to all places of interest in Snowdonia National Park and an ideal base for touring, walking and exploring. All rooms have colour TV, radio and hospitality trays. Most rooms en-suite. Hearty breakfasts. Packed lunches, snacks, evening meals. Special diets catered for by arrangement. Enjoy the peace and relaxed atmosphere. *i*

P	🚭	NIGHTLY B & B PER PERSON		WEEKLY D, B & B PER PERSON		🛏 5
						🛁 3
		MIN £ 18.00	MAX £ 20.00	MIN £ 193.00	MAX £ 207.00	OPEN 1 - 12

Welcome Host

Customer care is our top priority. It's what our Welcome Host scheme is all about. Welcome Host badge or certificate holders are part of a tradition of friendliness. The Welcome Host programme, which is open to everyone from hotel staff to taxi drivers, places the emphasis on warm Welsh hospitality and first-class service.

Betws-y-Coed Blaenau Ffestiniog Caernarfon Conwy

GH | Eirianfa Guest House

15-16 Castle Road,
Dolwyddelan,
Nr. Betws-y-Coed LL25 0NX
Tel: (01690) 750360
Fax: (01690) 750360

APPROVED

Homely guest house in Snowdonia National Park between Betws-y-Coed and Blaenau Ffestiniog. Relaxing guest lounge. Double or twin-bedded rooms. All en-suite, remote controlled satellite colour television, tea/coffee making facilities. Excellent home cooked meals, laundry/drying services. Central for touring Snowdonia, coastal resorts, slate mines. Ideal for trekking, hiking, climbing, fishing. Reductions: short breaks, weekly stay. Brochure awaiting. **i**

		NIGHTLY B & B PER PERSON		WEEKLY D, B & B PER PERSON		🛏 3
						🛁 3
		MIN £	MAX £	MIN £	MAX £	OPEN
		14.00	14.00	120.00	140.00	1 - 12

FGH | Ty Coch Farm & Trekking Centre

Penmachno,
Betws-y-Coed LL25 0HJ
Tel: (01690) 760248

AWARD

Set in lovely valley in hills. Six miles Betws-y-Coed. Excellent base for touring Snowdonia railways, , slate mines, castles. Golf, pony trekking available. Comfortable accommodation and friendly personal service. Many recommendations and return visits. Central heating, en-suite, tea making, guests' lounge with TV and video. SAE please or ring for details at any time. **i**

		NIGHTLY B & B PER PERSON		WEEKLY D, B & B PER PERSON		🛏 3
						🛁 3
		MIN £	MAX £	MIN £	MAX £	OPEN
		17.00	19.00	170.00	180.00	1 - 12

A Journey Through Wales

- **Magnificently produced book, the ideal gift or memento**
- **High quality photographs with accompanying text take you on a tour of Wales**
- **Classic views of Wales's scenic mountains and coastline**
- **A complete pictorial record - everything from powerful castles to colourful craft workshops, picturesque villages to narrow-gauge railways**

£5.10 inc. p&p

(see 'Get Yourself a Guide' at the end of the book)

H | Queens Hotel

1 High Street,
Blaenau Ffestiniog LL41 3ES
Tel: (01766) 830055
Fax: (01766) 830046

HIGHLY COMMENDED

Victorian hotel adjacent to Ffestiniog railway. Completely refurbished in 1996. Individually designed bedrooms. All en-suite. Spacious family rooms available. Bistro styled restaurant in evenings, (non-smoking). Bar meals available all day. Ideal centre for exploring Snowdonia's mountains and coastline, famous slate caverns, castles, Portmeirion, golf courses. Accessible by rail. **i**

		NIGHTLY B & B PER PERSON		WEEKLY D, B & B PER PERSON		🛏 12
						🛁 12
		MIN £	MAX £	MIN £	MAX £	OPEN
		25.00	35.00	230.00	300.00	1 - 12

H | Menai Bank Hotel

North Road,
Caernarfon LL55 1BD
Tel: (01286) 673297
Fax: (01286) 673297

HIGHLY COMMENDED

*Family owned period hotel, many original features. Extensive sea views, close to castle, Snowdonia. Tastefully decorated comfortable bedrooms, one ground floor, colour televisions, tea makers, clock radios, attractive restaurant, bar, residents lounge, pool table, car park, garden. Short breaks. Free castle pass - enquire for details. Credit cards accepted. Colour brochure. AA/RAC**.* **i**

		NIGHTLY B & B PER PERSON		WEEKLY D, B & B PER PERSON		🛏 15
						🛁 11
		MIN £	MAX £	MIN £	MAX £	OPEN
		16.00	25.50	195.30	261.45	1 - 12

FH | Pengwern Farm

Saron,
Llandwnda,
Caernarfon
LL54 5UH
Tel: (01286) 831500 Fax: (01286) 831500
Mobile: (0378) 411780

DE LUXE AWARD

Charming spacious farmhouse of character, beautifully situated between mountains and sea; unobstructed views of Snowdonia. Well appointed bedrooms, all en-suite. Land runs down to Foryd Bay, noted for its bird life. Jane Rowlands has a cookery diploma and provides excellent meals with farmhouse fresh food, using local produce. Excellent access. **i**

		NIGHTLY B & B PER PERSON		WEEKLY D, B & B PER PERSON		🛏 3
						🛁 3
		MIN £	MAX £	MIN £	MAX £	OPEN
		20.00	25.00	224.00	248.00	2 - 11

H | Castle Bank Hotel

Mount Pleasant,
Conwy LL32 8NY
Tel: (01492) 593888

HIGHLY COMMENDED

Well established hotel in mediaeval Conwy. AA Rosette for our meals, plus an RAC restaurant merit award. Ample parking within own grounds. High standards throughout. Totally non-smoking. Write or phone for brochure and sample menu and let us tell you more. **i**

		NIGHTLY B & B PER PERSON		WEEKLY D, B & B PER PERSON		🛏 9
						🛁 8
		MIN £	MAX £	MIN £	MAX £	OPEN
		26.50	-	245.00	-	2 - 12

H | The Lodge

Tal-y-Bont,
Nr. Conwy
LL32 8YX
Tel: (01492) 660766
Fax: (01492) 660534

   HIGHLY COMMENDED

We are a rather special well appointed family run hotel situated in the beautiful Conwy Valley. A perfect location for a short break or relaxing holiday and near to all the major attractions of the coast and Snowdonia, including Bodnant Garden. Friendly and attentive staff to whom nothing is too much trouble; wonderful food, with much produce from our own gardens. Ample parking. Good walking. Write or phone for colour brochure. *i*

	NIGHTLY B & B PER PERSON	WEEKLY D, B & B PER PERSON	🛏 10
			🛏 10
	MIN £	MAX £	MIN £	MAX £	OPEN
	25.00	30.00	235.00	270.00	1 - 12

FH | Henllys Farm

Llechwedd,
Conwy
LL32 8DJ
Tel: (01492) 593269

  HIGHLY COMMENDED

 AWARD

In the heart of beautiful countryside, ideally placed for touring Snowdonia, north Wales coast, Bodnant Garden and Anglesey. 1 1/2 miles from Conwy. Twin/double family bedrooms, both en-suite. Tea/coffee facilities, guest TV lounge. Good home cooking from fresh local produce. Homely peaceful accommodation. Ample secure parking. *i*

	NIGHTLY B & B PER PERSON	WEEKLY D, B & B PER PERSON	🛏 2
			🛏 2
	MIN £	MAX £	MIN £	MAX £	OPEN
	16.00	20.00	150.00	170.00	3 - 11

H | Min y Gaer Hotel

Porthmadog Road
Criccieth LL52 0HP
Tel: (01766) 522151
Fax: (01766) 523540

  HIGHLY COMMENDED

A pleasant licensed hotel, situated near the beach with delightful views of Criccieth Castle and the Cardigan Bay coastline. Ten comfortable, centrally heated rooms, all with colour TV and tea/coffee facilities. An ideal base for touring Snowdonia and the Llŷn Peninsula. Private car parking. AA Recommended. RAC Acclaimed. *i*

	NIGHTLY B & B PER PERSON	WEEKLY D, B & B PER PERSON	🛏 10
			🛏 9
	MIN £	MAX £	MIN £	MAX £	OPEN
	18.00	21.00	185.50	192.50	3 - 10

H | Tir-y-Coed Country House Hotel

Rowen,
Conwy LL32 8TP
Tel: (01492) 650219

 HIGHLY COMMENDED

A warm welcome awaits you here, four miles from historic Conwy in a picturesque Snowdonian village. Relax amidst beautiful mountainous scenery in peaceful surroundings. Within easy reach of coast, castles, gardens and stately homes. Well appointed en-suite bedrooms with magnificent views. Excellent home-cooked meals for all diets. Ample parking. *i*

	NIGHTLY B & B PER PERSON	WEEKLY D, B & B PER PERSON	🛏 7
			🛏 7
	MIN £	MAX £	MIN £	MAX £	OPEN
	22.50	26.00	225.00	246.00	3 - 11

H | Glyn y Coed Hotel

Porthmadog Road,
Criccieth LL52 0HP
Tel: (01766) 522870
Fax: (01766) 523341

  HIGHLY COMMENDED

AA/RAC acclaimed beautiful Victorian house overlooking sea, mountains, castles, close to Portmeirion. Highly recommended home cooking, catering for most diets. Private parking, cosy bar. En-suite bedrooms (one ground floor), colour TV, tea making facilities. Senior rates. Also self-catering sleeping 9. Excellent value and superior accommodation ensures perfect holiday. *i*

	NIGHTLY B & B PER PERSON	WEEKLY D, B & B PER PERSON	🛏 10
			🛏 10
	MIN £	MAX £	MIN £	MAX £	OPEN
	23.00	25.00	190.00	215.00	1 - 12

GH | Craig y Môr Guest House

West Parade,
Criccieth
LL52 0EN
Tel: (01766) 522830

   **HIGHLY COMMENDED**

From single persons to family groups, we welcome people of all ages for a relaxing holiday in our very comfortable, well appointed house overlooking Tremadog Bay. Meals, including special diets, follow our British tradition of using tasty, quality produce - local when available. Pets welcome. Detailed brochure sent on request from Arlene, Brian or Phil. *i*

	NIGHTLY B & B PER PERSON	WEEKLY D, B & B PER PERSON	🛏 6
			🛏 6
	MIN £	MAX £	MIN £	MAX £	OPEN
	19.00	21.00	197.05	208.95	3 - 10

Wales: Castles and Historic Places

- Beautifully produced full-colour guide to more than 140 historic sites
- Castles, abbeys, country houses, prehistoric and Roman remains
- Detailed maps

£7.25 inc. p&p
(see 'Get Yourself a Guide' at the end of the book)

Dinas Mawddwy Dolgellau

FH	Bryncelyn Farm

Dinas Mawddwy,
Machynlleth SY20 9JG
Tel: (01650) 531289

HIGHLY COMMENDED

A warm welcome awaits you at Bryncelyn Farm. Located in the peaceful valley of Cywarch, with beautiful unspoilt views. An excellent centre for walking, climbing and touring. Spacious en-suite bedrooms with tea/coffee making facilities, colour television and heating. Ideal base for touring Mid Wales, Snowdonia and seaside resorts. Five minutes away from main north to south road A470.

		NIGHTLY B & B PER PERSON		WEEKLY D, B & B PER PERSON		🛏 2
						🍽 2
		MIN £ 18.00	MAX £ –	MIN £ –	MAX £ –	OPEN 1 - 12

H	Clifton House Hotel

Smithfield Square,
Dolgellau LL40 1ES
Tel: (01341) 422554

COMMENDED

Centrally situated in an unspoilt market town. This small hotel offers the ideal base to explore Snowdonia. Home comforts, personal attention from proprietors Rob and Pauline Dix and excellent cuisine from our AA Rosette and Les Routiers Award winning cellar restaurant.

i

P ♟		NIGHTLY B & B PER PERSON		WEEKLY D, B & B PER PERSON		🛏 6
						🍽 4
		MIN £ 16.00	MAX £ 26.00	MIN £ 217.00	MAX £ 280.00	OPEN 3 - 10

H	Dolmelynllyn Hall

Ganllwyd,
Dolgellau LL40 2HP
Tel: (01341) 440273
Fax: (01341) 440273

HIGHLY COMMENDED

Totally non-smoking. Dolmelynllyn stands in 3 acres of carefully tended gardens surrounded by National Trust owned mountains and meadows. The tranquil, old-world atmosphere helps guests relax from the daily stresses of modern life. All the well-equipped bedrooms are decorated differently whilst the elegant sitting-room and cosy conservatory bar offer unpretentious comfort. The charming panelled dining-room with superb food as befits an AA Rosette. A very warm welcome awaits you.

i

P ♟		NIGHTLY B & B PER PERSON		WEEKLY D, B & B PER PERSON		🛏 10
						🍽 10
		MIN £ 40.00	MAX £ 57.50	MIN £ 345.00	MAX £ 455.00	OPEN 3 - 11

H	Dolserau Hall Hotel

Dolgellau LL40 2AG
Tel: (01341) 422522
Fax: (01341) 422400

HIGHLY COMMENDED

Peacefully located amidst the spectacular scenery of Snowdonia National Park and picturesque gardens. Excellent walking, riding and railways. Comfortable lounges, spacious en-suite bedrooms with superb views and a delightful restaurant. Resident proprietors Marion and Peter Kaye promise a warm welcome. Winners of AA Courtesy and Care Award 1996.

i

P		NIGHTLY B & B PER PERSON		WEEKLY D, B & B PER PERSON		🛏 15
						🍽 15
		MIN £ 39.50	MAX £ 39.50	MIN £ 255.00	MAX £ 325.00	OPEN 2 - 12

H	Fronoleu Farm Hotel

Tabor,
Dolgellau LL40 2PS
Tel: (01341) 422361
Fax: (01341) 422361

COMMENDED

Secretly secluded, overlooking the magnificent Mawddach Estuary stands Fronoleu. This homely family run converted farm hotel combines traditional Welsh warmth with modern excellence. Log fired lounges, four poster beds, harpist most evenings, award winning licensed restaurant (open to non-residents) enhance the ambience of Fronoleu's cosy, friendly atmosphere. Free fishing.

i

P		NIGHTLY B & B PER PERSON		WEEKLY D, B & B PER PERSON		🛏 10
						🍽 6
		MIN £ 18.00	MAX £ 22.50	MIN £ –	MAX £ –	OPEN 1 - 12

H	Royal Ship Hotel

Queens Square,
Dolgellau LL40 1AR
Tel: (01341) 422209

COMMENDED

*This extensively modernised hotel stands in the centre of Dolgellau with a fine view of Cader Idris. Most bedrooms en-suite .Family rooms available. Colour TV in bedrooms. Full colour brochure on request. AA**, RAC** Car park. Access and Barclaycard accepted. Robinsons traditional draught beers.*

i

P		NIGHTLY B & B PER PERSON		WEEKLY D, B & B PER PERSON		🛏 24
						🍽 18
		MIN £ 20.00	MAX £ 50.00	MIN £ 120.00	MAX £ 300.00	OPEN 1 - 12

GH | Ivy House

Finsbury Square,
Dolgellau LL40 1RF
Tel: (01341) 422535
Fax: (01341) 422689

`COMMENDED`

Country town guest house and restaurant offering attractive accommodation, welcoming atmosphere and good food. Cellar bar, lounge, full central heating. All rooms TV, tea and coffee facilities. Extensive menu of home prepared food, including several vegetarian dishes. "Taste of Wales" member. Perfect centre for touring and walking. *i*

		NIGHTLY B & B PER PERSON		WEEKLY D, B & B PER PERSON		6
						3
		MIN £	MAX £	MIN £	MAX £	OPEN
		18.00	24.00	-	-	1 - 12

GH | Einion House

Friog,
Fairbourne LL38 2NX
Tel: (01341) 250644

`COMMENDED`

Comfortable rooms, double, twin or single, en-suite available in lovely old house between mountains and sea. Beautiful scenery, staggering sunsets. Good home cooking. Marvellous walking, maps available. Pony trekking, fishing and birdwatching. Good centre for narrow gauge railways. Castles within easy reach. Safe sandy beach few minutes walk from house. All bedrooms colour TV, clock radios, hairdryers, teamakers. Vegetarians catered for. Write or phone now for full details and brochure pack. *i*

		NIGHTLY B & B PER PERSON		WEEKLY D, B & B PER PERSON		7
						4
		MIN £	MAX £	MIN £	MAX £	OPEN
		17.00	18.50	161.00	170.00	1 - 12

H | Victoria Inn

Llanbedr LL45 2LD
Tel: (01341) 241213

`COMMENDED`

Recently refurbished to the highest standard. This cosy inn now offers five en-suite bedrooms tastefully refurnished for your every comfort. The Victoria stands in the centre of the village on the banks of the River Artro. Delicious bar meals available. Colour TV in bedrooms. Robinsons traditional draught beers. *i*

	NIGHTLY B & B PER PERSON		WEEKLY D, B & B PER PERSON		5
					5
	MIN £	MAX £	MIN £	MAX £	OPEN
	26.00	26.00	-	-	1 - 12

H | The Fairbourne Hotel

Fairbourne LL38 2HQ
Tel: (01341) 250203

`COMMENDED`

Come and enjoy a lovely break in this 17th century hotel, renowned for its good food, friendly atmosphere and comfort. Log fires, well stocked bars. Situated opposite the estuary from Barmouth with commanding views of Cardigan Bay. All rooms have colour TV, tea making facilities. En-suites. Bowls green in grounds. Ideally situated for outdoor pursuits, pony trekking, sailing, climbing, golf, miniature railway. Brochure on request. *i*

		NIGHTLY B & B PER PERSON		WEEKLY D, B & B PER PERSON		23
						20
		MIN £	MAX £	MIN £	MAX £	OPEN
		27.50	29.00	235.00	256.00	1 - 12

H | Estuary Motel

Talsarnau LL47 6TA
Tel: (01766) 771155

`HIGHLY COMMENDED`

The motel with all the facilities of a hotel. Family run close by glorious beaches, beautiful mountain scenery, golf courses, fishing, riding, etc. Comfortable, Sky TV lounge, licensed bar, restaurant, with excellent evening meals. Ample car parking. Large discounts on three day breaks available. Telephone for brochure. *i*

		NIGHTLY B & B PER PERSON		WEEKLY D, B & B PER PERSON		10
						10
		MIN £	MAX £	MIN £	MAX £	OPEN
		20.00	23.00	156.00	200.00	1 - 12

H | Gwynedd Hotel

High Street,
Llanberis
LL55 4SU
Tel: (01286) 870203
Fax: (01286) 871636

`COMMENDED`

Set at the foot of Snowdon and opposite Lake Padarn with its magnificent surroundings, the Gwynedd is an ideal touring and walking base. There are eleven fully equipped guest rooms, most en-suite. The lounge bar provides a relaxing setting to enjoy a drink or bar meal, alternatively the elegant restaurant provides a comprehensive à la carte menu. *i*

		NIGHTLY B & B PER PERSON		WEEKLY D, B & B PER PERSON		11
						8
		MIN £	MAX £	MIN £	MAX £	OPEN
		18.00	24.00	220.00	230.00	1 - 12

Machynlleth Porthmadog

H	The Wynnstay Arms Hotel

Maengwyn Street,
Machynlleth SY20 8AE
Tel: (01654) 702941
Fax: (01654) 703884

 COMMENDED

The warmest welcome awaits at our 18th century former coaching inn. Comfortable, well appointed en-suite rooms. Excellent home cooked food served in our award winning restaurant. Luxurious lounges and cosy bar with our own home brewed real ales. Ideal base for touring, walking, fishing and so much more.

i

P 🅲 🚯 IIII. 🏋 🍴	NIGHTLY B & B PER PERSON		WEEKLY D, B & B PER PERSON		🛏 23 🍴 23
	MIN £	MAX £	MIN £	MAX £	OPEN
	27.50	-	225.00	-	1 - 12

GH	Skellerns

35 Madoc Street,
Porthmadog LL49 4BU
Tel: (01766) 512843

Friendly welcome for all. Excellent Welsh breakfasts or vegetarian breakfasts served. Heating, tea/coffee making facilities and TV in all bedrooms. Keys supplied. Special rates for children. Shops, buses, trains, cinema nearby. Ideally situated for visiting Portmeirion Italianate Village, Snowdonia mountains, Ffestiniog Steam Railway and Black Rock Sands. Open all year. Proprietor Mrs R Skellern.

i

🐕 IIII.	NIGHTLY B & B PER PERSON		WEEKLY D, B & B PER PERSON		🛏 3 🍴
	MIN £	MAX £	MIN £	MAX £	OPEN
	12.50	14.00	-	-	1 - 12

GH	Ty Newydd

30 Dublin Street,
Tremadog LL49 2RH
Tel: (01766) 512553

 COMMENDED

Three double and one family bedrooms with hot/cold, TV, tea making facilities. All mod cons. Private car park. Central to Ffestiniog railway, Snowdon, Butlins, Black Rock Sands, pony trekking with unspoilt countryside for nature trails and coastal walks. Situated one mile from Porthmadog.

i

P 🚯 IIII.	NIGHTLY B & B PER PERSON		WEEKLY D, B & B PER PERSON		🛏 4 🍴
	MIN £	MAX £	MIN £	MAX £	OPEN
	14.00	-	-	-	4 - 10

Cyclists and Walkers Welcome

Look out for the 'boot' and 'bike' symbols. They are displayed by places which have undertaken to provide features which cyclists and/or walkers always find welcome. These include drying facilities for wet clothes and boots, secure lockable areas for bikes, availability of packed lunches and so on. You'll even be greeted with a welcoming cup of tea or coffee on arrival!

FGH	Felin Crewi Watermill

Felin Crewi, Penegoes,
Machynlleth SY20 8NH
Tel: (01654) 703113

HIGHLY COMMENDED

Stay in this 16th century watermill which actually works and makes stoneground flour. Breakfast is served overlooking the millpond and millrace. There is a private garden for guests or they can enjoy the riverside walk and meet the numerous farm animals all within the grounds in this tranquil setting.

i

P 🚯 IIII.	NIGHTLY B & B PER PERSON		WEEKLY D, B & B PER PERSON		🛏 2 🍴 1
	MIN £	MAX £	MIN £	MAX £	OPEN
	18.00	22.00	-	-	1 - 12

Wales Tourist Map

- **Our best-selling map** - now with a new look
- **Detailed 5 miles/inch scale**
- **Wealth of tourist information**
- **14 specially devised car tours**
- **Town plans**

£2.00 inc. p&p

(see 'Get Yourself a Guide' at the end of the book)

Portmeirion Italianate Village

40

Talyllyn Railway

FGH Yoke House Farm

Pwllheli LL53 5TY
Tel: (01758) 612621

HIGHLY COMMENDED

A beautifully wooded drive welcomes you to this Georgian farmhouse on 290 acre working farm, where guests are invited to watch the milking, calf feeding etc. Tastefully furnished, the accommodation consists of 1 double and 1 twin bedded rooms, all with wash basins, shaver points and welcome tray. Exciting nature trail open to guests. Enjoy the tranquillity of a country farmhouse and be assured of a warm Welsh welcome.

P		NIGHTLY B & B PER PERSON		WEEKLY D, B & B PER PERSON		2
		MIN £	MAX £	MIN £	MAX £	OPEN
		16.50	17.00	-	-	4 - 10

H Fairy Falls Hotel

Trefriw LL27 0JU
Tel: (01492) 640250
Fax: (01492) 640250

 COMMENDED

Family run inn and hotel of great character, superbly situated in the heart of the Conwy Valley. Ideal for all beauty spots and places of interest. Renowned for excellent food and frequented by friendly locals and visitors all year round.

P	C	NIGHTLY B & B PER PERSON		WEEKLY D, B & B PER PERSON		6
		MIN £	MAX £	MIN £	MAX £	OPEN
		17.00	20.00	153.00	171.00	1 - 12

FGH Gesail Farm

Bryncrug,
Tywyn LL36 9TL
Tel: (01654) 782286

  HIGHLY COMMENDED

Beautiful farmhouse, situated at the foot of Bird-rock. Elegant rooms with separate lounge for guests. TV and beverage tray in all rooms. Outdoor heated swimming pool. Many attractions indoor and outdoor only short distance away. Excellent for walking, cycling, fishing and rock climbing. A true working farm.

P		NIGHTLY B & B PER PERSON		WEEKLY D, B & B PER PERSON		4
		MIN £	MAX £	MIN £	MAX £	OPEN
		16.00	17.50	196.00	-	1 - 12

41

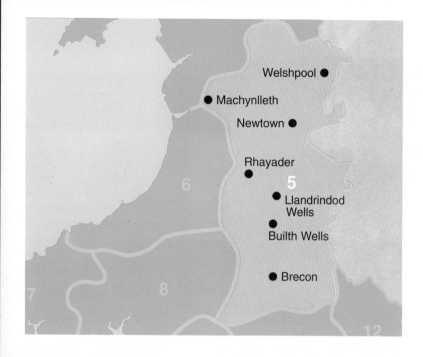

This large area encompasses the rural heartlands of Wales. From the unexplored Berwyn Mountains in the north to the grassy heights of the Brecon Beacons in the south, the predominant colour is green. And the predominant mood is restful, for this is Wales's most peaceful and unhurried area, a place of quiet country roads and small market towns, hill sheep farms and rolling borderlands. It's also a place of scenic lakes — the Elan Valley, Clywedog and Vyrnwy — set in undisturbed landscapes rich in wildlife, where you may spot the rare red kite circling in the skies. And Wales's great outdoors doesn't come any greater than in the Brecon Beacons National Park, whose wide, open spaces were made for walking and pony trekking.

It's a fact...

The Brecon Beacons National Park, covering 519 square miles, was designated in 1957. The Beacons' peak of Pen-y-fan, at 886m/2907ft, is the highest summit in South Wales. The Elan Valley reservoirs, created between 1892 and 1903, were the first of Wales's man-made lakelands. Llanwrtyd Wells appears in the Guiness Book of Records as the smallest town in Britain. 19th century diarist Francis Kilvert was curate of the Clyro in the 1860's and 70's. A stone in the church commemorates his association with the village. Sections of the 8th-century earthwork known as Offa's Dyke still stand almost to their full height in the hills around Knighton.

Ge6　Brecon

Main touring centre for the 519 square miles of the Brecon Beacons National Park. Handsome old town with thriving market, ruined castle, cathedral (with its imaginative Heritage Centre), priory, two interesting museums (Brecknock and South Wales Borderers') and Welsh Whisky Experience attraction. Wide range of inns and good shopping. Centre for walking and pony trekking. Golf, fishing, and canal cruising also available. Very popular summer International Jazz Festival.

Ge4　Builth Wells

Solidly built old country town which plays host every July to the Royal Welsh Agricultural Show, Wales's largest farming gathering. Lovely setting on River Wye amid beautiful hills. Lively sheep and cattle markets. Good shopping for local products, touring centre for Mid Wales and border country. River walk, Wyeside Arts Centre.

Hb7　Crickhowell

Small, pleasant country town beautifully situated on the River Usk. Good for walking, fishing, pony trekking and riding. Remains of Norman castle, Nearby 14th-century Tretower Court and earlier castle worth a visit.

Gc3　Elan Valley

The first – and possibly the most scenic – of Wales's man-made lakelands. A string of reservoirs set in high moor and mountain, an area rich in wildlife. Elan Valley Visitor centre at Elan village.

Hb5　Hay-on-Wye

Small market town on the Offa's Dyke Path, nestling beneath the Black Mountains on a picturesque stretch of the River Wye. A mecca for book lovers – there are antiquarian and second-hand bookshops, some huge, all over the town. Attractive crafts centre. Literature Festival in early summer attracts big names.

Ge3　Llandrindod Wells　⇌

Victorian spa town with spacious streets and impressive architecture. Victorian-style visitor centre and excellent museum tracing the history of spa. Magic Lantern Theatre. A popular inland resort with golf, fishing, bowling, boating and tennis available. Excellent touring centre for Mid Wales hills and lakes. Annual Victorian Festival in August.

Eb3　Llanfyllin

Historic small country town in rolling peaceful farmlands at head of scenic Cain Valley. Undisturbed borderlands all around. Nearby Lake Vyrnwy and 73m/240ft Pistyll Rhaeadr waterfall are popular beauty spots. Also close to Welshpool and Powis Castle.

Ec6　Montgomery

Hilltop market town of distinctive Georgian architecture beneath the ruins of a 13th-century castle. Offa's Dyke, which once marked the border, runs nearby. Not far from Welshpool and Powis Castle.

43

Eb6   Newtown   🚉

Busy Severn Valley market town and one-time home of Welsh flannel industry. Textile history recalled in small museum; another museum based around Robert Owen, pioneer socialist, who lived here. Town also has interesting W H Smith Museum, solid old buildings, river promenade, street market and the lively Theatr Hafren.

Ec5   Welshpool   🚉

Old market town of the borderlands, full of character, with half-timbered buildings and welcoming inns. Attractive canalside museum. Good shopping centre; golf and angling. Powis Castle is an impressive stately home with a Clive of India Museum and outstanding gardens. Ride the narrow-gauge Welshpool and Llanfair Light Railway, visit the Moors Wildlife Collection.

Eb3   Penybontfawr

Secluded village amid forest and lake, near the spectacular 73m/240ft Pistyll Rhaeadr waterfall. Pony trekking and walking country, with hills and woods all around. Lake Vyrnwy Visitor Centre nearby.

Welshpool & Llanfair Light Railway

Lake Vyrnwy (Top)

H The Castle of Brecon Hotel

The Castle Square,
Brecon LD3 9DB
Tel: (01874) 624611
Fax: (01874) 623737

COMMENDED

An historic hotel, enjoying extensive views of the Brecon Beacons yet close to the centre of this ancient and attractive market town. The Castle, well known for its good food and friendly service, is ideally situated for exploring the landscape and attractions of South and Mid Wales.

		NIGHTLY B & B PER PERSON		WEEKLY D, B & B PER PERSON		🛏 45
						🛁 45
		MIN £	MAX £	MIN £	MAX £	OPEN
		30.00	40.00	-	237.00	1 - 12

H Nant Ddu Lodge Hotel

Cwm Taf,
Nr. Merthyr Tydfil CF48 2HY
Tel: (01685) 379111
Fax: (01685) 377088

HIGHLY COMMENDED

The Nant Ddu Lodge Hotel is a true country hotel and inn. Unfussy and family run, warm, welcoming and utterly relaxing. Yet guests sacrifice nothing in terms of comfort and surroundings, with the individually designed rooms rivalling the views which look out across the hotel's extensive lawns.

i

		NIGHTLY B & B PER PERSON		WEEKLY D, B & B PER PERSON		🛏 16
						🛁 16
		MIN £	MAX £	MIN £	MAX £	OPEN
		25.00	35.00	-	-	1 - 12

H Old Castle Farm Hotel

Llanfaes,
Brecon LD3 8DG
Tel: (01874) 622120

HIGHLY COMMENDED

The hotel is an old farmhouse which dates back to the 17th century. It is situated in the Brecon Beacons National Park area on the west side of the old market town of Brecon, half a mile from town centre and within easy reach of Beacons and Mountain Centre.

i

		NIGHTLY B & B PER PERSON		WEEKLY D, B & B PER PERSON		🛏 10
						🛁 10
		MIN £	MAX £	MIN £	MAX £	OPEN
		20.00	25.00	183.00	197.00	2 - 11

H The Olde Masons Arms Hotel

Hay Road,
Talgarth,
Brecon LD3 0BB
Tel: (01874) 711688

HIGHLY COMMENDED

Charming 16th century hotel with oak beams and country cottage ambience. Ideally situated for walking among the Black Mountains and Brecon Beacons National Park. Enjoy a warm welcome, excellent food in the "Taste of Wales" restaurant and relax in the friendly atmosphere of the lounge bar.

i

		NIGHTLY B & B PER PERSON		WEEKLY D, B & B PER PERSON		🛏 6
						🛁 6
		MIN £	MAX £	MIN £	MAX £	OPEN
		25.50	25.50	220.00	220.00	1 - 12

DISCOVERING ACCESSIBLE WALES

This publication is packed full of helpful information for visitors with disabilities.
Subjects covered include
attractions, accommodation
and activities.
For your free copy please see the
'Guides' section of this book.

H Tai'r Bull Inn

Libanus,
Brecon LD3 8EL
Tel: (01874) 625849

HIGHLY COMMENDED

Situated in a small rural village surrounded by beautiful countryside. Close to Mountain Centre, Pen-y-fan, waterfalls, pony trekking and much more. All rooms are en-suite in our oak beamed bar or dining room. Easy to find, just 3 miles out of Brecon on A470 towards Cardiff. Ideal walking and touring base.

i

		NIGHTLY B & B PER PERSON		WEEKLY D, B & B PER PERSON		🛏 5
						🛁 5
		MIN £	MAX £	MIN £	MAX £	OPEN
		19.00	19.00	-	-	1 - 12

GH The Beacons Guest House

16 Bridge Street,
Brecon LD3 8AH
Tel: (01874) 623339
Fax: (01874) 623339

COMMENDED

Characterful, georgian house with cellar bar, lounge and private parking. Comfortable rooms, mostly en-suite with many "extras". Four poster and king size luxury rooms also available. Excellent Aga-cooked food - "Taste of Wales" recommended. Ideally situated just two minutes walk to the town centre, cathedral, museums, canal, marina and salmon river. Many local attractions and outdoor activities available on the doorstep. Credit cards accepted. Ring Peter or Barbara Jackson for further information.

i

		NIGHTLY B & B PER PERSON		WEEKLY D, B & B PER PERSON		🛏 10
						🛁 7
		MIN £	MAX £	MIN £	MAX £	OPEN
		16.50	24.50	165.00	215.00	1 - 12

Brecon Builth Wells Crickhowell

GH | The Coach Guest House

Orchard Street,
Brecon LD3 8AN
Tel: (01874) 623803

HIGHLY COMMENDED

"Hotel standards at guest house prices". All six bedrooms are en-suite, three with bath, three with shower and have colour TV, hairdryer, clock/radio, telephone and beverage tray. Whole house completely non smoking. Ideal base for touring Brecon Beacons National Park. RAC Highly Acclaimed. AA listed QQQQ.

P ♿ 🍴	NIGHTLY B & B PER PERSON		WEEKLY D, B & B PER PERSON		🛏 6 🛏 6
	MIN £	MAX £	MIN £	MAX £	OPEN
	19.00	20.00	–	–	1 - 12

FH | Lodge Farm

Talgarth,
Brecon
LD3 ODP
Tel: (01874) 711244
Fax: (01874) 711244

HIGHLY COMMENDED

Comfortable 18th century farmhouse nestling in the Black Mountains, 1¹/2 miles out of Talgarth off A479 in the eastern part of the Brecon Beacons National Park. The house enjoys mountain views set in large garden where guests are welcome to relax. Well appointed cosy rooms, period furniture, oak beamed dining room with original inglenook fireplace and flagstone floor. Freshly prepared food, including vegetarian is a speciality. Come explore the delights of this beautiful area. Hay-on-Wye 8 miles. Brochure.

P ♿ 🍴	NIGHTLY B & B PER PERSON		WEEKLY D, B & B PER PERSON		🛏 3 🛏 3
	MIN £	MAX £	MIN £	MAX £	OPEN
	17.50	19.00	182.00	-	1 - 12

H | Pencerrig Gardens Hotel

Llandrindod Road,
Builth Wells LD2 3TF
Tel: (01982) 553226
Fax: (01982) 552347

COMMENDED

Set in beautiful gardens, Pencerrig is the perfect place to relax and do nothing except be pampered by the warmest of Welsh hospitality. It is an ideal starting point for holidays of all kinds, with excellent golf, fishing, walking and much more, within easy reach. The hotel has twenty en-suite bedrooms, all with telephones, colour televisions and tea makers to ensure your stay is made as comfortable as possible.

P 🐕 ♿ 🍴	NIGHTLY B & B PER PERSON		WEEKLY D, B & B PER PERSON		🛏 20 🛏 20
	MIN £	MAX £	MIN £	MAX £	OPEN
	25.00	37.50	258.00	270.00	1 - 12

FGH | Disserth Mill

Disserth,
Builth Wells LD2 3TN
Tel: (01982) 553217

250 metres off A483, 3 miles North of Builth Wells, 2¹/2 miles to Royal Welsh show ground. Picturesque area for walking. 13 miles to Elan Valley, reservoirs, Woollen Mill, Brecon Beacons National Park. Washbasins, TV, tea/coffee facilities in all bedrooms. Quiet garden to relax in.

P 🐕 ♿ 🍴	NIGHTLY B & B PER PERSON		WEEKLY D, B & B PER PERSON		🛏 3 🛏
	MIN £	MAX £	MIN £	MAX £	OPEN
	15.00	16.00	161.00	161.00	4 - 10

FGH | New Hall Farm Guest House

Llanddewircwm,
Builth Wells
LD2 3RX
Tel: (01982) 552483

HIGHLY COMMENDED

AWARD

Situated 1¹/2 miles from Builth Wells market town and Royal Welsh Showground. Magnificent unspoilt scenery overlooking the Wye Valley and Aberedw hills. Picturesque walking area, paragliding, mountain biking. Centrally situated for all places and activities in central Wales. Easy access to parking, comfortable accommodation in 17th century farmhouse renovated to a high standard. Good home cooked meals, personal welcome and services from proprietor. Ground floor bedrooms. Brochure available.

P ♿ 🍴	NIGHTLY B & B PER PERSON		WEEKLY D, B & B PER PERSON		🛏 5 🛏 3
	MIN £	MAX £	MIN £	MAX £	OPEN
	16.00	20.00	168.00	196.00	1 - 12

H | Stables Hotel

Llangattock,
Crickhowell NP8 1LE
Tel: (01873) 810244

HIGHLY COMMENDED

High class internationally known country hotel. Magnificent position in 30 acres garden and grounds. RAC Acclaimed. All rooms en-suite. Restaurant with Wales's largest fireplace. Our speciality superb cooking with fresh local produce. All main meals served with six fresh vegetables. New - Trelawney suites - four poster beds and conservatory rooms.

P 🐕 ♿ 🍴	NIGHTLY B & B PER PERSON		WEEKLY D, B & B PER PERSON		🛏 14 🛏 14
	MIN £	MAX £	MIN £	MAX £	OPEN
	25.00	30.00	245.00	-	1 - 12

Award-winning farmhouses and guest houses

Look out for the Wales Tourist Board Award on the pages of this guide. Award winners offer extra-special standards of comfort, furnishings and surroundings. They're as good as many a hotel. And proprietors will have completed a tourism training course covering most aspects of running an accommodation enterprise.

AWARD

Crickhowell Elan Valley Hay-on-Wye Llandrindod Wells

H	Ty Croeso Hotel

The Dardy,
Llangattock,
Crickhowell NP8 1PU
Tel: (01873) 810573
Fax: (01873) 810573

HIGHLY COMMENDED

Originally part of Victorian workhouse, now a delightful country hotel in the Brecon Beacons National Park with magnificent views over the Black Mountains and Usk Valley. Renowned for delicious food - speciality "Taste of Wales" menu, also à la carte and vegetarian menus available. A warm welcome with log fires and attentive, friendly service. All rooms are en-suite and charmingly decorated. Prime walking location. Ideal base for visiting many historical and tourist attractions. **i**

	NIGHTLY B & B PER PERSON		WEEKLY D, B & B PER PERSON		🛏 8
					🛁 8
	MIN £	MAX £	MIN £	MAX £	OPEN
	27.50	32.50	250.00	295.00	1 - 12

H	Elan Valley Hotel

Elan Valley,
Nr Rhayader LD6 5HN
Tel: (01597) 810448

COMMENDED

Relaxed family run Victorian hotel in spectacular unspoilt lakeland of Wales. Perfect base for walking, fishing, cycling, red kite watching. 2 miles charming town of Rhayader with excellent leisure facilities. Renowned for our delicious food, freshly cooked with flair and imagination, and our friendly, lively atmosphere. Children made very welcome. **i**

	NIGHTLY B & B PER PERSON		WEEKLY D, B & B PER PERSON		🛏 10
					🛁 10
	MIN £	MAX £	MIN £	MAX £	OPEN
	22.50	30.00	170.00	260.00	1 - 12

H	The Famous Old Black Lion

Lion Street,
Hay-on-Wye HR3 5AD
Tel: (01497) 820841

HIGHLY COMMENDED

A 13 century inn, famous for its cuisine. Situated in the famous book town of Hay-on-Wye. Situated on the medieval old town wall 200 to 300 yards from the centre of the town, but yet in a quiet spot, full of old beamy character and style with own game fishing.

i

	NIGHTLY B & B PER PERSON		WEEKLY D, B & B PER PERSON		🛏 10
					🛁 10
	MIN £	MAX £	MIN £	MAX £	OPEN
	21.00	24.00	270.00	300.00	1 - 12

GH	The Old Post Office

Llanigon,
Hay-on-Wye HR3 5QA
Tel: (01497) 820008

COMMENDED

Grade II listed 17th century character house in quiet rural location, only two miles from the famous book town Hay-on-Wye. Set in the lovely Brecon Beacons National Park at the foot of the Black Mountains. Offa's Dyke path close by. Superb vegetarian breakfast early or late. Relaxed atmosphere. Guests' own sitting room and lovely bedrooms.

i

	NIGHTLY B & B PER PERSON		WEEKLY D, B & B PER PERSON		🛏 3
					🛁 2
	MIN £	MAX £	MIN £	MAX £	OPEN
	16.00	21.00	–	–	2 - 12

Pets welcome

You'll see from the symbols that many places to stay welcome dogs and pets by prior arrangement. Although some sections of beach may have restrictions, there are always adjacent areas - the promenade, for example, or quieter stretches of sands - where dogs can be exercised on and sometimes off leads. Please ask at a Tourist Information Centre for advice.

H	Llanerch 16th Century Inn

Llanerch Lane,
Llandrindod Wells
LD1 6BG
Tel: (01597) 822086
Fax: (01597) 824618

COMMENDED

Traditional atmosphere and hospitality with modern day comforts. Bedrooms have colour TV, radio, telephone, tea/coffee facilities and en-suite. Excellent selection of meals, good traditional ales, good wine list, beer garden terrace, children's play area. Close to town centre and set in its own grounds. Families welcome, plenty of parking.

i

	NIGHTLY B & B PER PERSON		WEEKLY D, B & B PER PERSON		🛏 12
					🛁 12
	MIN £	MAX £	MIN £	MAX £	OPEN
	22.50	24.50	200.00	225.00	1 - 12

Wales Tourist Map
* Our best-selling map - now with a new look
* Detailed 5 miles/inch scale
* Wealth of tourist information
* 14 specially devised car tours
* Town plans

£2.00 inc. p&p
(see 'Get Yourself a Guide' at the end of the book)

H	The Park Motel

Crossgates,
Llandrindod Wells LD1 6RF
Tel: (01597) 851201
Fax: (01597) 851201

COMMENDED

Set in 3 acres, amidst beautiful countryside yet conveniently situated on the A44. The centrally heated units are available for bed and breakfast or self-catering. Self contained, en-suite, twin bedded room, fully fitted kitchenette, sleeps 4. Colour television, tea and coffee making facilities, radio alarm clock. Fully licensed restaurant, lounge bar. Pets welcome.

i

	NIGHTLY B & B PER PERSON		WEEKLY D, B & B PER PERSON		🛏 7
					🛁 7
	MIN £	MAX £	MIN £	MAX £	OPEN
	18.00	23.00	153.00	178.00	2 - 12

Llandrindod Wells Llanfyllin

GH	Corven Hall

Howey,
Llandrindod Wells
LD1 5RE
Tel: (01597) 823368

HIGHLY COMMENDED

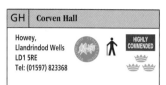

Victorian country house with large grounds in peaceful setting.1¹/2 miles south of Llandrindod Wells, off A483 at Hundred House turn. The house is licensed, centrally heated and spacious. Large dining room, TV lounge, bar. Most bedrooms en-suite, TV, tea/coffee facilities. Ground floor accommodation, traditional cooking, home-made and freshly prepared. Ample parking. Beautiful countryside. Elan Valley, Brecon Beacons, River Wye nearby. Brochure Rod and Beryl Prince. *i*

		NIGHTLY B & B PER PERSON		WEEKLY D, B & B PER PERSON		🛏 10
						🛁 8
		MIN £	MAX £	MIN £	MAX £	OPEN
		17.00	19.00	154.00	164.00	2 - 10

FH	Brynhir Farm

Chapel Road,
Howey,
Llandrindod Wells
LD1 5PB
Tel: (01597) 822425

HIGHLY COMMENDED AWARD

Charming olde worlde farmhouse situated 1 mile off A483 in magnificent mountain setting. Traditional inglenook fireplace, exposed oak beams. Ideal relaxing holiday, good walking area, trout fishing, lake pied flycatchers, redstarts, buzzards and owls commonly seen, conducted badger sett tours. En-suite rooms, beverage tray, delicious cuisine. Conservation and rural tourism award. Ground floor accommodation. Woollen mills, River Wye, Elan Valley, mountain lakes, Brecon Beacons National Park all nearby. Pets welcome. Large car park. SAE brochure Mrs Nixon. *i*

		NIGHTLY B & B PER PERSON		WEEKLY D, B & B PER PERSON		🛏 6
						🛁 6
		MIN £	MAX £	MIN £	MAX £	OPEN
		17.00	18.00	165.00	180.00	3 - 11

FH	Cyfie Farm

Llanfihangel-
yng-Ngwynfa,
Llanfyllin SY22 5JE
Tel/Fax: (01691) 648451
Central Res. (01691) 870346

DE LUXE AWARD

A wonderful place to holiday, close to the fairy tale landscape of Lake Vyrnwy. De luxe farmhouse in magnificent setting. Spacious barn and stable suites offer the comforts of a top hotel. Other cosy bedrooms. Log fired lounges, peace, tranquillity. A real "Taste of Wales" in hospitality and cuisine. Working Farm. *i*

		NIGHTLY B & B PER PERSON		WEEKLY D, B & B PER PERSON		🛏 4
						🛁 4
		MIN £	MAX £	MIN £	MAX £	OPEN
		20.00	26.50	201.00	237.00	1 - 12

Powis Castle, near Welshpool

Prices

Please note that all prices are **PER PERSON**, based on **TWO PEOPLE** sharing a double or twin room. **SINGLE OCCUPANCY** will usually be charged extra, and there may be supplements for private bath/shower. All prices include VAT. Daily rates are for bed and breakfast. Weekly rates are for dinner, B&B. Please check all prices and facilities before confirming your booking.

H	Dragon Hotel

Montgomery
SY15 6PA
Tel: (01686) 668359
Fax: (01686) 668359

This quiet 17th century family run hotel in the lee of Montgomery Castle boasts an excellent restaurant offering the best of local produce and a warm personal welcome to all. Indoor heated swimming pool. All bedrooms en-suite, some non-smoking. Nearby there are opportunities for fishing, shooting, golf and visits to historic sites. *i*

		NIGHTLY B & B PER PERSON		WEEKLY D, B & B PER PERSON		🛏 15
						🛏 15
		MIN £	MAX £	MIN £	MAX £	OPEN
		34.50	36.00	209.65	279.95	1 - 12

FH	Lower Gwestydd

Newtown
SY16 3AY
Tel: (01686) 626718

HIGHLY COMMENDED
AWARD

Lower Gwestydd is a beautiful half timbered 17th century listed farmhouse. Just off the B4568 north of Newtown. 2 rooms en-suite centrally heated. Tea/coffee facilities. Separate dining room with large inglenook. Lounge with colour TV. Large garden with lovely views. Warm welcome at this 200 acre working farm. Ideal for walking, fishing, golf etc., close by. *i*

		NIGHTLY B & B PER PERSON		WEEKLY D, B & B PER PERSON		🛏 2
						🛏 2
		MIN £	MAX £	MIN £	MAX £	OPEN
		18.00	19.00	180.00	190.00	1 - 12

Please Note

All the accommodation in this guide has applied for grading. However, at the time of going to press not all establishments had been visited - some of these properties are indicated by the wording '**Awaiting Grading**'.

GH	Blaen Hirnant Guest House

Hirnant,
Penybontfawr,
Nr Oswestry SY10 0HR
Tel: (01691) 870330

HIGHLY COMMENDED

14th century Welsh farmhouse, peacefully situated in Montgomeryshire hills. Tastefully renovated exposing original cruck beam construction., Inglenook fireplace. En-suite rooms have TV/radio, tea/coffee, central heating. Comfortable Lounge. Oak beamed dining room. Pre-booked dinner available, special diets catered for. Lake Vyrnwy 3 mile walk! Bird watching, walking, central for touring. Wherever and whatever you choose to do the scenery is a joy in itself. Within easy reach are Powis Castle, Chirk Castle, Snowdonia and more! *i*

		NIGHTLY B & B PER PERSON		WEEKLY D, B & B PER PERSON		🛏 3
						🛏 3
		MIN £	MAX £	MIN £	MAX £	OPEN
		15.00	16.50	-	175.00	1 - 12

FGH	Tynllwyn Farm

Welshpool
SY21 9BW
Tel: (01938) 553175

HIGHLY COMMENDED

Tynllwyn is a family run farm with a warm friendly welcome. Good farmhouse food and service. 1 mile from the lovely market town of Welshpool on the A490 north - stands on a hillside, very quiet and pleasantly situated with beautiful views of the Severn Valley and Long Mountain. All bedrooms have colour TV, tea/coffee making facilities. Bar licence and fire certificate. "Taste of Wales" Member. *i*

		NIGHTLY B & B PER PERSON		WEEKLY D, B & B PER PERSON		🛏 3
						🛏 1
		MIN £	MAX £	MIN £	MAX £	OPEN
		15.00	17.50	-	-	1 - 12

Slide Sets

Ask about our attractive range of 35mm colour slides showing views of Wales, available at 75p per slide. For a complete list of subjects please contact the Photographic Librarian, Wales Tourist Board, Davis Street, Cardiff CF1 2FU (tel 01222-475215).

WALES CYMRU

A DIFFERENT HOLIDAY EVERY DAY

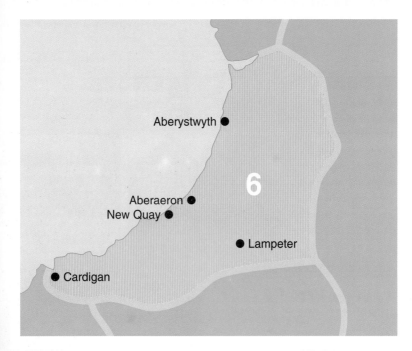

The southern arc of Cardigan Bay is dotted with pretty little ports and resorts, the largest of which is Victorian Aberystwyth with its splendid seafront. Long sections of this seashore have been designated Heritage Coast, including the exposed headland of Ynys Lochtyn near Llangrannog where on stormy days it almost seems as if you are sailing away from the mainland on board a ship. Inland, you'll discover traditional farming country matched by traditional country towns. Venture a little further and you'll come to the Cambrian Mountains, a compelling wilderness area crossed only by the occasional mountain road. The Teifi Valley, in contrast, is a gentle, leafy landscape famous for its beautiful river scenery, falls and coracle fishing.

It's a fact...

Dylan Thomas took much of his inspiration for the fictitious seatown of Llareggub in *Under Milk Wood* from New Quay. Remote Strata Florida Abbey, Pontrhydfendigaid, was known as the 'Westminster Abbey of Wales' in medieval times. Aberystwyth's Cliff Railway, opened in 1896, is Britain's longest electric-powered cliff railway. The scenic Teifi Valley was once Wales's busiest woollen making area – a few mills still survive. Cardigan Bay's bottlenose blue dolphin population is one of only two known to reside in UK coastal waters.

Fe2   Aberystwyth   ⇌

Premier resort on the Cardigan Bay coastline. Fine promenade, cliff railway, camera obscura, harbour and many other seaside attractions. Excellent museum in restored Edwardian theatre. University town, lively arts centre with theatre and concert hall. National Library of Wales stands commandingly on hillside. Good shopping. Vale of Rheidol narrow-gauge steam line runs to Devil's Bridge falls.

Fa5   Cardigan

Market town on mouth of River Teifi close to beaches and resorts. Good shopping facilities, accommodation, inns. Golf and fishing. Base for exploring inland along wooded Teifi Valley and west to the Pembrokeshire Coast National Park. Y Felin Corn Mill and ruined abbey at neighbouring St Dogmael's. Welsh Wildlife Centre nearby.

Fe5   Lampeter

Farmers and students mingle in this distinctive small country town in the picturesque Teifi Valley. Concerts are often held in St David's University College, and visitors are welcome. Golf and angling, range of small shops and some old inns. Visit the landscaped Cae Hir Gardens, Cribyn.

Fc4   New Quay

Picturesque little resort with old harbour on Cardigan Bay. Lovely beaches and coves around and about. Good for sailing and fishing. Resort sheltered by protective headland.

Fb5   Rhydlewis

Country village set in peaceful Cardiganshire farmlands. Good base for exploring Teifi Valley to the south and Cardigan Bay to the north. Spectacular coast at Llangrannog only a few miles away.

Ga3   Tregaron

Small traditional market town with good pony trekking. Anglers and naturalists delight in this area – the great bog nearby is a nature reserve with rare flowers and birds. Wildlife centre at nearby Penuwch. On the doorstep of remote uplands – follow the old drovers' route across the spectacular Abergwesyn Pass.

Llyn Brianne

Llangrannog (top)

Aberystwyth Cardigan

H	Conrah Country House Hotel

Chancery,
Aberystwyth
SY23 4DF
Tel: (01970) 617941
Fax: (01970) 624546

  HIGHLY COMMENDED

Discreet Welsh country hotel only minutes from the spectacular cambrian coast and university town of Aberystwyth. Tucked away amid woodlands and gardens. An atmosphere of quiet luxury pervades. Restaurant renowned for award winning cuisine and fine wines. Leisure facilities include a small indoor heated swimming pool. *i*

	NIGHTLY B & B PER PERSON		WEEKLY D, B & B PER PERSON		🛏 20
					🛁 20
MIN £	MAX £	MIN £	MAX £	OPEN	
44.00	55.00	348.00	414.00	1 - 12	

H	Llety Gwyn Hotel

Llanbadarn Fawr,
Aberystwyth SY23 3SX
Tel: (01970) 623965

APPROVED

Llety Gwyn family hotel, 1¹/2 miles sea front A44. Most rooms en-suite, doubles, twin, family, single rooms, colour TV, tea making, radios all rooms, ground floor bedrooms, ramps. Pleasant garden, swings, river walk in own grounds. Public bar, pool table, large car park. Access, Visa, American Express. Warm Welsh welcome from the Jones family AA Gwesty Croesawgar gyda Cymru Cymraeg. *i*

	NIGHTLY B & B PER PERSON		WEEKLY D, B & B PER PERSON		🛏 14
					🛁 8
MIN £	MAX £	MIN £	MAX £	OPEN	
20.00	28.00	–	–	1 - 12	

Slide Sets

Ask about our attractive range of 35mm colour slides showing views of Wales, available at 75p per slide. For a complete list of subjects please contact the Photographic Librarian, Wales Tourist Board, Davis Street, Cardiff CF1 2FU (tel 01222-475215).

H	Allt-y Rheini Mansion Hotel

Cilgerran,
Nr. Cardigan SA43 2TJ
Tel: (01239) 612286

HIGHLY COMMENDED

Informal family run hotel set in 4¹/2 acres of grounds overlooking beautiful countryside and only 5 minutes from local beaches. Most rooms en-suite, colour TV and tea/coffee making facilities. Relax in the lounge or take a drink in our conservatory bar. Restaurant offers traditional Welsh fayre and traditional home cooking. Putting green and croquet lawn. Children welcome. Plenty of car parking. "Taste of Wales" member. *i*

	NIGHTLY B & B PER PERSON		WEEKLY D, B & B PER PERSON		🛏 8
					🛁 5
MIN £	MAX £	MIN £	MAX £	OPEN	
27.00	27.00	245.00	245.00	1 - 12	

Aberystwyth

H | Penbontbren Farm Hotel

HIGHLY COMMENDED

lynarthen,
ardigan SA44 6PE
el: (01239) 810248
ax: (01239) 811129

astefully converted pine furnished stone buildings
vo miles from Cardigan Bay. Excellent cuisine.
amily rooms offer colour TV, direct dial telephone,
athroom, heating, hot drinks tray, rural views.
mall bar, residents lounge, occasional harp music.
ttractions include farm museum/crafts, nature trail.
argain breaks available. Ground floor rooms for
isabled. "Taste of Wales" member. AA/RAC**.

i

	NIGHTLY B & B PER PERSON		WEEKLY D, B & B PER PERSON		🛏 10
					🛁 10
	MIN £	MAX £	MIN £	MAX £	OPEN
🍴	34.00	37.00	322.00	343.00	1 - 12

Award-winning farmhouses and guest houses

Look out for the **Wales Tourist Board Award** on the pages of this guide. Award winners offer extra-special standards of comfort, furnishings and surroundings. They're as good as many a hotel. And proprietors will have completed a tourism training course covering most aspects of running an accommodation enterprise.

AWARD

w Quay

FH | Brynog Mansion

HIGHLY COMMENDED

Felinfach,
Lampeter
SA48 8AQ
Tel: (01570) 470266

Spacious 250 year old mansion. Situated in the beautiful Vale of Aeron, midway between Lampeter University town and the unique Aberaeron seaside resort, 15 minutes by car. Approached by 0.75 miles rhododendron lined drive off the A482 main road and village of Felinfach. 2 spacious en-suite bedrooms, other near bathroom, tea making facilities, central heating. Full breakfast served in the grand old furnished dining room. *i*

P	🚽	NIGHTLY B & B PER PERSON		WEEKLY D, B & B PER PERSON		🛏 3
						🛁 2
		MIN £	MAX £	MIN £	MAX £	OPEN
		18.00	19.00	-	-	1 - 12

DISCOVERING ACCESSIBLE WALES

**This publication is packed full of helpful information for visitors with disabilities.
Subjects covered include attractions, accommodation and activities.
For your free copy please see the 'Guides' section of this book.**

FGH | Tŷ Hen Farm

COMMENDED

Llwyndafydd
SA44 6BZ,
Tel: (01545) 560346

Peaceful and secluded 18th century farmhouse set on a working sheep farm. En-suite rooms with colour TV and drink making facilities. Licensed bar. Private complex includes a large indoor heated pool, sauna, fitness room, sunbed, skittles, etc. Ideally situated for both walking and touring. Close to heritage coastal path and numerous bays, beaches. No smoking. *i*

P	🐴	NIGHTLY B & B PER PERSON		WEEKLY D, B & B PER PERSON		🛏 2
🏆						🛁 2
	🍴	MIN £	MAX £	MIN £	MAX £	OPEN
		20.00	29.00	POA	POA	2 - 10

FH | Llwyn-yr-Eos

HIGHLY COMMENDED

Rhydlewis,
Llandysul SA44 5QU
Tel: (01239) 851268

Enjoy beautiful views, peace and tranquillity, and good food on our sheep farm in the Teifi Valley. Guests have their own sitting room with a log fire for chilly evenings. Ideal for walking, bird watching or just relaxing and only 10 minutes drive from safe, sandy beaches. Children welcome. Please send for brochure. *i*

P	🍴	NIGHTLY B & B PER PERSON		WEEKLY D, B & B PER PERSON		🛏 2
	🍴					🛁 2
		MIN £	MAX £	MIN £	MAX £	OPEN
		17.50	17.50	172.50	186.50	1 - 12

GH | Neuaddlas Country Guest House

Tregaron SY25 6LE
Tel: (01974) 298905

HIGHLY COMMENDED

Well established country guest house, central for coast and countryside. Overlooking Cors Caron Nature Reserve. Much wildlife and many walks nearby. A warm welcome awaits our guests - home cooking, log fires and comfortable accommodation, all adds up to a relaxing holiday - one visit is never enough! Experience our unique Welsh hospitality. Informative brochure available on request. *i*

P	🐴	NIGHTLY B & B PER PERSON		WEEKLY D, B & B PER PERSON		🛏 6
C	🚽					🛁 3
	🍴	MIN £	MAX £	MIN £	MAX £	OPEN
		16.50	21.00	175.00	195.00	1 - 12

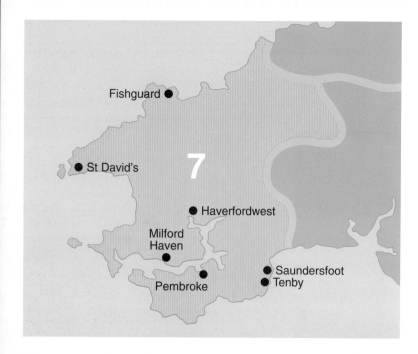

Pembrokeshire is traditionally known as *gwlad hud a lledrith*, 'the land of magic and enchantment'. Anyone who has visited the sandy bays around Tenby, for example, or the breathtaking sea-cliffs at Stack Rocks, or the rugged coastline around St David's will agree with this description. Pembrokeshire is one of Europe's finest stretches of coastal natural beauty. Not surprisingly, it's also a haven for wildlife. Wildflowers grow on its cliffs, seals swim in its clear waters, and seabirds nest in huge numbers all along the coast. Pembrokeshire's stunning coastal beauty extends inland to the Preseli Hills, an open expanse of highland scattered with mysterious prehistoric sites. And away from the coast you'll also discover castles and a host of places to visit.

It's a fact...

The Pembrokeshire Coast National Park created in 1952, covers 225 square miles, from Poppit Sands in the north to Amroth in the south. The Pembrokeshire Coast Path, opened in 1970, runs for 186 miles. The Dale Peninsula is the sunniest place in Wales. The last invasion of British soil took place at Carreg Wastad beach in 1797 - an event which will be re-enacted in 1997 as part of the celebrations planned to commemorate the invasion's bicentenary.

Jb5 Broad Haven

Sand and green hills cradle this holiday village on St Bride's Bay in the Pembrokeshire Coast National Park. Beautiful beach and coastal walks. National Park Information Centre.

Jb3 Croes-goch

Small village, useful spot for touring Pembrokeshire Coast National Park – especially its peaceful, rugged northern shores and nearby centres of St David's and Fishguard. Llangloffan Farmhouse Cheese Centre nearby.

Jb6 Dale

Sheltered yachting village at mouth of Milford Haven Waterway. Henry VII landed near here and marched on to take the crown at the Battle of Bosworth in 1485. Many good beaches nearby. Skokholm and Skomer islands offshore – both marvellous havens for seabirds.

Jc2 Fishguard ≥

Lower Fishguard is a cluster of old wharfs and cottages around a beautiful harbour. *Under Milk Wood* with Richard Burton was filmed here in 1971. Shopping in Fishguard town. Good walks along Pembrokeshire Coast Path and in the country. Nearby Goodwick is the Irish ferry terminal, with a direct link from London. Excellent range of craft workshops in area including Tregwynt Woollen Mill. Music Festival in July.

Jc5 Haverfordwest ≥

Ancient town – now a good base for exploring the Pembrokeshire Coast National Park – and the administrative and shopping centre for the area. Medieval churches and narrow streets. Museum in the castle grounds, which occupy an outcrop overlooking the town. Attractive redeveloped riverside and old wharf buildings. Picton Castle a few miles to the east. Many other attractions nearby, including Scolton Manor Country Park, 'Motormania' exhibition, Selvedge Farm Museum and Nant-y-Coy Mill.

Jb5 Little Haven ≥

Combines with Broad Haven – just over the headland to form a complete family seaside holiday centre in the Pembrokeshire Coast National Park. The village dips down to a pretty sandy beach. Popular spot for sailing, swimming and surfing.

Jb5 Marloes

Village near Marloes Sands, a remote stretch of the Pembrokeshire Coast National Park – and one of its finest beaches – overlooking Skomer Island, a haven for puffins and other seabirds. Good swimming and surfing; boat trips to the island from nearby Martin's Haven.

Je5 Narberth ≥

Small market town, ancient castle remains (private). Charming local museum. Convenient for beaches of Carmarthen Bay and resorts of Tenby and Saundersfoot. Many attractions nearby, including activity-packed Oakwood Park, Canaston Centre, Heron's Brook Country Park, Folly Farm and Blackpool Mill.

Jd2 Newport

Ancient castled village on Pembrokeshire coast. Fine beaches – bass and sea trout fishing. Pentre Ifan Burial Chamber is close by. Backed by heather-clad Preseli Hills and overlooked by Carn Ingli Iron Age Fort.

Jd6 Pembroke

Ancient borough built around Pembroke Castle, birthplace of Henry VII. In addition to its impressive castle, well-preserved sections of old town walls. Fascinating Museum of the Home. Sandy bays within easy reach, yachting, fishing – all the coastal activities associated with estuaries. Plenty of things to see and do in the area, including visit to beautiful Upton Castle Grounds.

Ja4 St David's

Smallest cathedral city in Britain, shrine of Wales's patron saint. Magnificent ruins of a Bishop's Palace beside ancient cathedral nestling in hollow. Set in Pembrokeshire Coast National Park, with fine beaches nearby; superb scenery on nearby headland. Craft shops, sea life centres, painting courses, boat trips to Ramsey Island, farm parks and museums; ideal for walking and birdwatching.

Je6 Saundersfoot

Very attractive resort and sailing centre on the south Pembrokeshire coast within the national park. Good sandy beach and pretty harbour filled with colourful holiday craft. Excellent sea fishing. Tenby and a host of places to visit nearby, including Folly Farm, a family attraction based at a large working farm.

Jb6 Solva

Pretty Pembrokeshire coast village with small perfectly sheltered harbour and excellent craft shops. Pembrokeshire Coast Path offers good walking. Famous cathedral at nearby St David's.

Je6 Tenby

Popular, picturesque south Pembrokeshire resort with two wide beaches. Fishing trips from the attractive Georgian harbour and boat trips to nearby Caldy Island. The medieval walled town has a maze of charming narrow streets and fine old buildings, including Tudor Merchant's House (National Trust). Galleries and craft shops, excellent museum on headland, good range of amenities. Attractions include Manor House Wildlife and Leisure Park and Silent World Aquarium.

Tenby

Broad Haven Croes-goch Dale Fishguard

FH	The Bower Farm

Little Haven,
Haverfordwest
SA62 3TY
Tel: (01437) 781554

HIGHLY COMMENDED
AWARD

Family farmhouse run by local historic family. Fantastic views over St. Brides Bay, offshore islands and Coast Path. Fine country cuisine. Pets and children welcome. Walking distance of sandy beaches. Safe parking. Lots of quiet animals and birds. Previous visitor's comment, "This is something special". Recommended by "Holiday Which?" and "Daily Mail". **i**

P ⫞	NIGHTLY B & B PER PERSON	WEEKLY D, B & B PER PERSON	🛏 4
			🛁 4

MIN £	MAX £	MIN £	MAX £	OPEN
18.00	25.00	210.00	280.00	1 - 12

FGH	Trearched Farm Guest House

Croes-goch,
Haverfordwest
SA62 5JP
Tel: (01348) 831310
Fax: (01348) 831310

HIGHLY COMMENDED

Enjoy a relaxing break in our 18th century listed farmhouse on arable farm. Long drive entrance by Y Lodge on A487 at village outskirts. Spacious grounds with small lake. Double, twin or single rooms for B&B. Ideal walking, birdwatching. Footpath link to coast at Trefin, approximately 2¼ miles. **i**

P ⫞	NIGHTLY B & B PER PERSON	WEEKLY D, B & B PER PERSON	🛏 6
			🛁

MIN £	MAX £	MIN £	MAX £	OPEN
15.00	15.00	-	-	1 - 12

H	The Post House Hotel

Dale,
Haverfordwest,
SA62 3RE
Tel: (01646) 636201

HIGHLY COMMENDED

Family run licensed hotel. 100 yards from sea and water sports centre in National Park coastal village of Dale. Area of outstanding natural beauty and close to Bird Islands of Skokholm and Skomer. Five en-suite bedrooms, one suite. All individually heated and courtesy tray. Tastefully furnished. Our suite has twin beds, comfortable lounge with television overlooking the meadow and sea. Residents' lounge. Large conservatory. Pleasant dining room and bar. Closed February. **i**

P ⫞	NIGHTLY B & B PER PERSON	WEEKLY D, B & B PER PERSON	🛏 5
			🛁 5

MIN £	MAX £	MIN £	MAX £	OPEN
20.00	25.00	195.00	235.00	1 - 12

Please Note

All the accommodation in this guide has applied for grading. However, at the time of going to press not all establishments had been visited - some of these properties are indicated by the wording 'Awaiting Grading'.

GH	Rhos Felen

Scleddau,
Fishguard SA65 9RD
Tel: (01348) 873711
Fax: (01348) 873711

HIGHLY COMMENDED

Family run country house in 3 acres. Putting green. 2 miles from Fishguard and Goodwick (Irish ferry and BR). Ideal base for coastal path, beaches, Preseli hills and St. David's. Guest lounge with colour TV. Home cooking in our adjoining restaurant, including vegetarian and special diets. Family room and self-contained 2 bedroom unit (double and twin with private bathroom, both sleeping 4/5). Late ferry bookings. **i**

P ⫞	NIGHTLY B & B PER PERSON	WEEKLY D, B & B PER PERSON	🛏 3
			🛁 1

MIN £	MAX £	MIN £	MAX £	OPEN
16.00	19.00	169.00	189.00	1 - 12

H	The Cartref Hotel

15/19 High Street,
Fishguard SA65 9AW
Tel: (01348) 872430
Fax: (01348) 872430

APPROVED

The Cartref Hotel is a pleasant town hotel in the centre of Fishguard providing comfortable rooms with TV and coffee/tea making facilities, some en-suite. The licensed restaurant serves home cooked meals with a continental flavour at a reasonable price. The hotel is convenient for shops, pubs, ferry port, and scenic walks. It is a good base for exploring the beautiful countryside around Fishguard. **i**

P ⫞	NIGHTLY B & B PER PERSON	WEEKLY D, B & B PER PERSON	🛏 12
			🛁 6

MIN £	MAX £	MIN £	MAX £	OPEN
17.50	27.00	172.00	191.00	1 - 12

GH	Glanmoy Lodge

Tref-wrgi Road,
Goodwick,
Fishguard SA64 OJX
Tel: (01348) 874333
Fax: (01348) 874333

HIGHLY COMMENDED

Free, one night when booking seven. Enjoy a restful stay with us. Privacy, peace and quiet guaranteed. Secure parking. All bedrooms en-suite, double, twin, family or six person accommodation. Lovely setting in spacious grounds. Choice of breakfasts and times. Tea, coffee always available. All amenities. Ferry and beaches one mile. Late night travellers welcome. **i**

P ⫞	NIGHTLY B & B PER PERSON	WEEKLY B & B PER PERSON	🛏 3
			🛁 3

MIN £	MAX £	MIN £	MAX £	OPEN
16.00	20.00	96.00	120.00	1 - 12

Award-winning farmhouses and guest houses

Look out for the Wales Tourist Board Award on the pages of this guide. Award winners offer extra-special standards of comfort, furnishings and surroundings. They're as good as many a hotel. And proprietors will have completed a tourism training course covering most aspects of running an accommodation enterprise.

AWARD

Fishguard Haverfordwest

GH	Heathfield

Mathry Road,
Letterston,
Haverfordwest SA62 5EG
Tel: (01348) 840263

HIGHLY COMMENDED

Our exclusive Georgian country house in its tranquil setting of pastures and woodlands is the perfect place to relax and be spoilt. It is ideally situated to explore all of Pembrokeshire's treasures. The comfortable spacious guest rooms with beautiful views over rolling countryside, the friendly atmosphere and the excellent food and wines will make your holiday truly enjoyable.

P ⚲ 🏠	NIGHTLY B & B PER PERSON		WEEKLY D, B & B PER PERSON		🛏 3
					3
MIN £	MAX £	MIN £	MAX £		OPEN
18.00	20.00	170.00	180.00		4 - 10

H	Wolfscastle Country Hotel

Wolf's Castle,
Haverfordwest SA62 5LZ
Tel: (01437) 741688/741225
Fax: (01437) 741383

HIGHLY COMMENDED

The hotel is a member of Welsh Rarebits, The Welsh Gold Collection of independently owned hotels and is situated amidst the beautiful Pembrokeshire scenery in close proximity to the bays, harbours, hills and splendid National Park coastline. Well known locally for good, home cooked cuisine at reasonable prices. The hotel is renowned for its atmosphere and comfortable surroundings.

P 🏠	NIGHTLY B & B PER PERSON		WEEKLY D, B & B PER PERSON		🛏 20
					20
MIN £	MAX £	MIN £	MAX £		OPEN
35.00	40.00	245.00	280.00		1 - 12

GH	Austalise

Keeston Hill,
Camrose,
Haverfordwest SA62 6EJ
Tel: (01437) 710303

HIGHLY COMMENDED

Modern guest house surrounded by lawns and flower borders. In elevated position with panoramic views of countryside within easy reach of many sandy beaches, golf course, fun park, marvellous coastal walks. 20 minutes Irish ferry. Free parking within grounds.

P 🏠	NIGHTLY B & B PER PERSON		WEEKLY D, B & B PER PERSON		🛏 5
					5
MIN £	MAX £	MIN £	MAX £		OPEN
17.50	17.50	-	-		1 - 12

FH	Cuckoo Mill Farm

Pelcomb Bridge,
St Davids Road,
Haverfordwest SA62 6EA
Tel: (01437) 762139

Ideally situated peacefully in central Pembrokeshire on working family farm, two miles from Haverfordwest. Ten minutes drive to coastline walks, sandy beaches, golf course, riding stables. Real home comfort in pretty heated rooms, H&C, tea trays, radio. Good home cooked meals. Evening meal reductions for senior citizens and children. Personal attention.

P 🏠	NIGHTLY B & B PER PERSON		WEEKLY D, B & B PER PERSON		🛏 3
					1
MIN £	MAX £	MIN £	MAX £		OPEN
15.00	17.50	145.00	165.00		1 - 12

Prices

In this publication we go to great lengths to make sure that you have a clear, accurate idea of prices and facilities. It's all spelled out in the 'Prices' sections - and remember to confirm everything when making your booking.

FH	Headland Farm

Ambleston,
Haverfordwest SA62 5QX
Tel: (01348) 881255

HIGHLY COMMENDED

Our family dairy farm is ideally situated in the heart of Pembrokeshire, surrounded by the rolling Preseli Hills. A paradise for walkers. Fishing at Llys-y-fran Dam, golf, horse riding, within easy reach. Good home cooking with a warm and friendly welcome, tea/coffee facilities in tastefully decorated bedrooms. Reductions for children and senior citizens.

P 🏠 🍴	NIGHTLY B & B PER PERSON		WEEKLY D, B & B PER PERSON		🛏 2
					.
MIN £	MAX £	MIN £	MAX £		OPEN
15.00	17.50	145.00	160.00		3 - 10

FH	Knock Farm

Camrose,
Haverfordwest SA62 6HW
Tel: (01437) 762208

HIGHLY COMMENDED

Our working daily farm is peacefully situated in a scenic valley in central Pembrokeshire, ten minures from Pembrokeshire's sandy beaches and coastline walks, two miles from Haverfordwest. Ideally situated for fishing, horse riding, walking, golf. Tasty home cooking, homely atmosphere, pretty centrally heated bedrooms, tea/coffee facilities, large family bedroom en-suite. Reductions children and senior citizens.

P 🏠 🍴	NIGHTLY B & B PER PERSON		WEEKLY D, B & B PER PERSON		🛏 3
					1
MIN £	MAX £	MIN £	MAX £		OPEN
15.00	17.50	145.00	165.00		3 - 10

Little Haven Marloes Narbeth Newport Pembroke

GH Whitegates

Little Haven,
Haverfordwest SA62 3LA
Tel: (01437) 781552
Fax: (01437) 781386

COMMENDED

Country house style accommodation overlooking lovely fishing village and St. Bride's Bay. Most rooms with sea views and private facilities, ideal for walking coastal path, bird watching islands, golf, riding, or beach holidays, warm welcome awaits you. Several excellent eating places within easy walking distance. Heated swimming pool in season. ℹ️

P 🐕 🛇 🍴 🏠		NIGHTLY B & B PER PERSON		WEEKLY D, B & B PER PERSON		🛏 3 🛁 3
		MIN £ 20.00	MAX £ -	MIN £ 245.00	MAX £ –	OPEN 1 - 12

FGH Highland Grange Farm Guest House

Robeston Wathen,
Narberth SA67 8EP
Tel: (01834) 860952

COMMENDED

Central location on A40 amidst beautiful countryside. Ideal touring centre, panoramic views, pleasant walks. Light and spacious well appointed ground floor accommodation. Two en-suites. Large guest lounge, comfort assured. Delicious home cooking using garden produce. Beach 8 miles, country Inn 200 yards, Oakwood Park 2 miles. Child reductions, helpful host. 1/2 hour to ferryports to Ireland. ℹ️

P C 🛇 🔥 🍴		NIGHTLY B & B PER PERSON		WEEKLY D, B & B PER PERSON		🛏 4 🛁 2
		MIN £ 14.50	MAX £ 18.00	MIN £ 146.50	MAX £ 170.00	OPEN 1 - 12

GH Grove Park Guest House

Pen-y-Bont,
Newport
SA42 0LT
Tel: (01239) 820122

HIGHLY COMMENDED

Grove Park is situated on the outskirts of Newport, one hundred yards from Pembrokeshire Coastal Path. 19th century house which has been completely refurbished but retains original character. Estuary views, easy distance from large sandy beach and Preseli Hills. Imaginative four course dinner menu, vegetarians welcome. Winter breaks. Log fires, colour TV all bedrooms. "Taste of Wales" member. ℹ️

P 🐕 🍴		NIGHTLY B & B PER PERSON		WEEKLY D, B & B PER PERSON		🛏 4 🛁 2
		MIN £ 19.50	MAX £ 21.50	MIN £ POA	MAX £ POA	OPEN 1 - 12

GH Foxdale Guest House

Glebe Lane,
Marloes,
Haverfordwest
SA62 3AY
Tel: (01646) 636243

HIGHLY COMMENDED

Large comfortable detached family house on the fringe of Marloes village. En-suite facilities, fully licensed and guests' TV lounge, tea/coffee all rooms. Close to cliff path, Skomer, Skokholm and Grassholm bird islands. Nearby Marloes sands, ideal base for bird watching, all water sports and walking to enjoy the spectacular coastal scenery and wild flowers. ℹ️

P 🐕 🏠		NIGHTLY B & B PER PERSON		WEEKLY D, B & B PER PERSON		🛏 4 🛁 1
		MIN £ 16.00	MAX £ 20.00	MIN £ -	MAX £ -	OPEN 1 - 12

H The Salutation Inn

Felindre Farchog,
Crymych SA41 3UY
Tel: (01239) 820564

COMMENDED

Beautifully situated in the Pembrokeshire Coast National Park. 5 minutes from Newport beach and Preseli Hills. Facilities nearby include riding, golf, fishing, sailing, birdwatching, walking, canoeing and lazing quietly. Modern and traditional rooms with tea/coffee making facilities. Pleasant restaurant, good food. A really relaxing place to stay. ℹ️

P 🐕 🛇 🔥 🍴		NIGHTLY B & B PER PERSON		WEEKLY D, B & B PER PERSON		🛏 9 🛁 9
		MIN £ 19.00	MAX £ 28.00	MIN £ 220.00	MAX £ 242.00	OPEN 1 - 12

H The Coach House Hotel

116 Main Street,
Pembroke SA71 4HN
Tel: (01646) 684602
Fax: (01646) 687456

HIGHLY COMMENDED

Traditional coaching inn situated in the picturesque castle town of Pembroke. Tastefully refurbished to provide 14 comfortable en-suite bedrooms. Enjoy delicious cuisine in Griffins Bistro beside an open log fire or snacks and cream teas in The Artists' Gallery upstairs. Gardens slope gently to the millpond where the medieval town walls are clearly visible. AA**. ℹ️

P 🐕 C 🛇 🏠 🍴		NIGHTLY B & B PER PERSON		WEEKLY D, B & B PER PERSON		🛏 14 🛁 14
		MIN £ 25.00	MAX £ 30.00	MIN £ 224.00	MAX £ 259.00	OPEN 1 - 12

St David's Saundersfoot

H	Old Cross Hotel

Cross Square,
St David's
SA62 6SP
Tel: (01437) 720387
Fax: (01437) 720394

HIGHLY COMMENDED

Centrally situated, quiet hotel, 1 minute from cathedral precinct, with a long standing reputation for good food, excellent accommodation and friendly service at reasonable prices. Private parking. Special diets catered for, vegetarian options. All rooms with modern facilities. An ideal base for walking, touring, birdwatching, botany or just relaxing. *i*

P	C	NIGHTLY B & B PER PERSON	WEEKLY D, B & B PER PERSON	🛏 16
				🛁 16
🛏	🍴	MIN £ 30.00	MAX £ 36.00	MIN £ 295.00	MAX £ 340.00	OPEN 3 - 12

H	Whitesands Bay Hotel

St David's SA62 6PT
Tel: (01437) 720403
or (01437) 720297
Fax: (01437) 720403

COMMENDED

Wales's most westerly hotel in quiet parkland setting, panoramic views over Whitesand Bay, St David's Head and Ramsey Island. Close to coastal path and environmentally clean beach, concessional green fees, several local golf courses, swimming pool, sauna, solarium. Many art galleries, potteries and craft centres within easy reach, also historical sites and water sports. Boat trips in locality, cathedral two miles. Excellent food and wines in restaurant and licensed bars. Short breaks off season. *i*
Ord. Survey No. SN 7365 2658.

P	🐕	NIGHTLY B & B PER PERSON	WEEKLY D, B & B PER PERSON	🛏 15
🛏				🛁 15
🍴		MIN £ 28.00	MAX £ 37.00	MIN £ 283.50	MAX £ 321.50	OPEN 1 - 12

H	Bay View Hotel

Pleasant Valley
Stepaside,
Saundersfoot
SA67 8LR
Tel: (01834) 813417

COMMENDED

Small family hotel with friendly atmosphere. Children really welcome. Situated in its own private peaceful surroundings away from crowded places, within easy reach of numerous beaches and delightful walks. Nearest beach 1/2 mile. Saundersfoot 1 1/2 miles, Tenby 5 miles. Some rooms en-suite. Cots, highchairs, babysitting, washing facilities. Crazy golf, mini golf, swings, outdoor heated swimming pool. Entertainment weekly in main season. TV lounge, residential licence, lunchtime snacks available. Ample parking. Brochure from Jean and Mike Artingstall.

P	🍴	NIGHTLY B & B PER PERSON	WEEKLY D, B & B PER PERSON	🛏 11
				🛁 8
		MIN £ 14.50	MAX £ 18.50	MIN £ 130.00	MAX £ 165.00	OPEN 4 - 9

St David's Cathedral

Saundersfoot Solva Tenby

H	Merlewood Hotel

St. Brides Hill,
Saundersfoot
SA69 9NP
Tel: (01834) 812421
Fax: (01834) 812421

COMMENDED

*Set in peaceful surroundings with own garden and superb views of Saundersfoot beach and village. Food cooked by resident proprietors, table d'hôte menu. Heated swimming pool, play area, mini golf, launderette. Entertainment main season. Rooms en-suite with TV, tea maker, radio baby listening. Family suites available. 5 minutes from village and beach. Ample car parking. Colour brochure available. AA/RAC**.* **i**

	NIGHTLY B & B PER PERSON	WEEKLY D, B & B PER PERSON	🚲 28
			🛏 28

MIN £	MAX £	MIN £	MAX £	OPEN
20.00	27.00	195.00	235.00	4 - 11

FGH	Lochmeyler Farm

Llandeloy,
Nr. Solva,
Haverfordwest
SA62 6LL
Tel: (01348) 837724
Fax: (01348) 837622

DE LUXE
AWARD

Warm welcome awaits you at Lochmeyler, 220 acre Dairy Farm Centre, St. David's Peninsula. Luxury facilities, including some 4 poster beds. Bedrooms have video and TV - large free video library with all latest films for use in rooms. National Park Activity Pack in each bedroom to help you explore our beautiful coast and countryside. No smoking in bedrooms. Two lounges, one for smokers. Pets and children welcome. Credit cards accepted. **i**

	NIGHTLY B & B PER PERSON	WEEKLY D, B & B PER PERSON	🚲 12
			🛏 12

MIN £	MAX £	MIN £	MAX £	OPEN
15.00	25.00	200.00	220.00	1 - 12

H	The Royal Gate House Hotel

North Beach,
Tenby SA70 7ET
Tel: (01834) 842255
Fax: (01834) 842441

Tenby - the jewel in the crown of the principality of Wales. Superb views of all Tenby's North Beach and harbour. All bedrooms en-suite with colour TV, telephone, courtesy trays, and baby listening. Parking, children's terms. Leisure complex with indoor pool. Catering for all types of holidays - including bargain breaks. Colour brochure. **i**

	NIGHTLY B & B PER PERSON	WEEKLY D, B & B PER PERSON	🚲 59
			🛏 59

MIN £	MAX £	MIN £	MAX £	OPEN
32.00	38.00	264.00	306.00	1 - 12

Call in at a Tourist Information Centre

Wales's network of TICs helps you get the best out of your holiday

- Information on what to see and where to go
- Local events
- Bed-booking service
- Brochures, maps and guides

It's so easy when you call in at a TIC

H	The Court Hotel

Lamphey,
Pembroke
SA71 5NT
Tel: (01646) 672273
Fax: (01646) 672480

DE LUXE

One of Wales's leading country hotels. Beautifully restored georgian mansion in quiet grounds near coast, renowned for award winning food and warm hospitality. Spacious bedrooms - complemented by attractive courtyard studios - ideal for families, children share free. Superb leisure centre, swimming pool, jacuzzi, gym, saunas, tennis, beautician. Corporate and business rates. Conference suites. A Best Western hotel. **i**

	NIGHTLY B & B PER PERSON	WEEKLY D, B & B PER PERSON	🚲 37
			🛏 37

MIN £	MAX £	MIN £	MAX £	OPEN
37.50	62.50	277.00	460.00	1 - 12

GH	Belle Vista

St. Florence,
Nr. Tenby
SA70 8LP
Tel: (01834) 871301

HIGHLY COMMENDED

Enjoy the comfort and luxury of a holiday in the well appointed bungalow home of Belle and Joe. Serenely rural, on the outskirts of picturesque village, with easy access to all amenities. Safe parking. Excellent varied home cooking. Morning tea/coffee tray. Outstanding hospitality and service. Regret no children or pets. Telephone/write for brochure. **i**

	NIGHTLY B & B PER PERSON	WEEKLY D, B & B PER PERSON	🚲 3
			🛏 3

MIN £	MAX £	MIN £	MAX £	OPEN
16.00	18.00	156.00	170.00	4 - 9

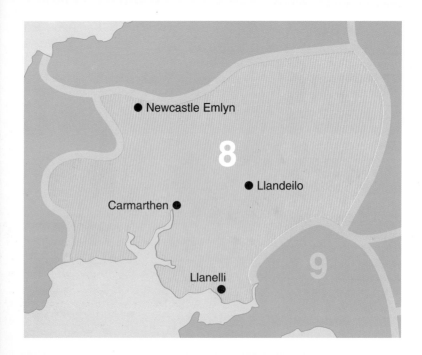

Dylan Thomas captured the essence of this timeless part of Wales in his short stories and poems, but most of all in his masterwork, *Under Milk Wood*. Dylan lived at Laugharne, a sleepy seatown set amongst the sweeping sands of Carmarthen Bay. Here you can wander along endless beaches, and then turn your attention to the patchwork of green farmlands which roll gently down to the sea. There's a rare sense of peace and tranquillity in the countryside around Carmarthen. Explore the lovely Vale of Towy, the moors of Mynydd Llanybydder or the glades of the Brechfa Forest. And don't miss market day at Carmarthen, or the view from the ramparts of Carreg Cennen, one of Wales's most spectacular castles.

It's a fact…

In the 1920s, the huge 6-mile beach at Pendine was used for land speed record attempts. Dolaucothi, Pumsaint, is the only place in Britain where we know, for certain, that the Romans mined for gold. The beach at Cefn Sidan, Pembrey, is 7 miles long. Twm Shôn Cati, Wales's answer to Robin Hood, hid in the hills north of Llandovery from the Sheriff of Carmarthen. Christmas mail can be postmarked from Bethlehem, a hamlet between Llandeilo and Llangadog.

Ke2 Ammanford ⇌

Bustling valley town, good for Welsh crafts and products, on western edge of Brecon Beacons National Park. Spectacular mountain routes over nearby Black Mountain to Llangadog.

Kc2 Carmarthen ⇌

Prosperous country town in pastoral Vale of Towy. Lively market and shops, livestock market. Carmarthen Castle was an important residence of the native Welsh princes but only the gateway and towers remain. Golf, fishing, tennis and well-equipped leisure centre. Remains of Roman amphitheatre. Immaculate museum in beautiful historic house on outskirts of town. Gwili Railway and ornamental Middleton Hall Amenity Area nearby.

Kd4 Llanelli ⇌

Bustling town with good shopping, covered market and pleasant parklands. Wildfowl and Wetlands Centre on estuary modelled on Slimbridge. Pembrey Country Park, adjoining 7 miles of sandy beach, has a visitor centre and many attractions including pony trekking, ski slope, adventure playground. The Welsh Motor Sports Centre and Kidwelly Castle and Industrial Museum are nearby.

Kc2 Llangain

Peaceful little settlement in rolling farmlands between Carmarthen and Llansteffan. Towy Estuary nearby, together with the evocative sandy shores of Carmarthen Bay which inspired writer Dylan Thomas.

Gb6 Llandovery ⇌

An important market town on the A40 with a ruined castle, good craft shops and excellent local museum/information centre; its Welsh name Llanymddyfri means the church among the waters . In the hills to the north is the cave of Twm Shôn Cati the Welsh Robin Hood. Good touring centre for Brecon Beacons and remote Llyn Brianne area.

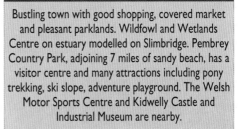

The Towy Estuary from Llansteffan Castle

Wildfowl and Wetlands Centre, near Llanelli (top)

Ammanford Carmarthen Llandovery

FGH | Bryncoch Farm

Llandyfan,
Ammanford SA62 2TY
Tel: (01269) 850480
Fax: (01269) 850480

COMMENDED

Bryncoch Farm, built in the 17th century, is situated high above the Amman Valley in the Brecon Beacons National Park. Golf course and riding centre only minutes away. Hosts Mary and Graham Richardson offer large comfortably furnished bedrooms, having en-suite bathrooms and unspoilt views over the valley. English breakfast cooked by your host is served in a warm and friendly atmosphere and is sure to set you up for the day.

	NIGHTLY B & B PER PERSON	WEEKLY D, B & B PER PERSON	🛏 3
	MIN £	MAX £	MIN £	MAX £	🛁 3
	15.00	-	-	-	OPEN 1 - 12

Carmarthen on the River Towy

FH | Plas Farm

Llangynog,
Carmarthen
SA33 5DB
Tel: (01267) 211492

COMMENDED

Working farm run by the Thomas family for almost a century. Conveniently situated six miles from Carmarthen along A40 west towards St.Clears quiet location. Ideal touring base one hour's drive from Fishguard, Pembroke and Irish Ferry. Ample safe parking, spacious farmhouse, en-suite available, tea making tray. Welcome assured.

	NIGHTLY B & B PER PERSON	WEEKLY D, B & B PER PERSON	🛏 3
	MIN £	MAX £	MIN £	MAX £	🛁 2
	15.00	17.00	–	–	OPEN 1 - 12

Wales Tourist Map
- Our best-selling map - now with a new look
- Detailed 5 miles/inch scale
- Wealth of tourist information
- 14 specially devised car tours
- Town plans

£2.00 inc. p&p

(see 'Get Yourself a Guide' at the end of the book)

H | The Castle Hotel

Kings Road,
Llandovery SA20 OAW
Tel: (01550) 720343
Fax: (01550) 720673

AWAITING GRADING

This typically Welsh market and historic town where the A40 crosses the Towy river is the perfect centre for the Brecon Beacons, the Black Mountains, the Cambrian wilderness, and is only 30 miles from the coast. Our important coaching inn overlooking the castle ruins is famous for family hospitality, good food and service. Now proud to represent Minotel in Mid Wales.

	NIGHTLY B & B PER PERSON	WEEKLY B, B & B PER PERSON	🛏 26
	MIN £	MAX £	MIN £	MAX £	🛁 14
	25.00	35.00	POA	POA	OPEN 1 - 12

H | Glanrannell Park Country House Hotel

Crugybar,
Llanwrda
SA19 8SA
Tel: (01558) 685230
Fax: (01558) 685784

HIGHLY COMMENDED

Ten miles west of Llandovery, lovely secluded hotel - a haven of peace. A wonderful centre for West and Mid Wales. Family run for 29 years with reputation for quality informal service, good food, fine wine and a warm welcome. Our colour brochure is only a phone call away.

	NIGHTLY B & B PER PERSON	WEEKLY B, B & B PER PERSON	🛏 8
	MIN £	MAX £	MIN £	MAX £	🛁 8
	28.00	32.00	308.00	-	OPEN 4 - 10

GH	Pen-y-Bont

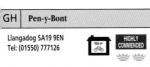

Llandadog SA19 9EN
Tel: (01550) 777126

HIGHLY COMMENDED

Charming guest house in tranquil streamside setting, fringe Brecon Beacons National Park, comfortable lounge separate dining room and pretty bedrooms. All rooms have private bath. Strong emphasis on excellent cuisine (trout, salmon etc). Tea making facilities. Ideally situated for exploring mountains, lakes and coastal areas. Glorious scenery, abundant wildlife and peace and quiet.

P		NIGHTLY B & B PER PERSON		WEEKLY D, B & B PER PERSON			3
		MIN £	MAX £	MIN £	MAX £	OPEN	3
		19.00	19.00	210.00	210.00	1 - 12	

FH	Cwmgwyn Farm

Llandadog Road,
Llandovery SA20 0EQ
Tel: (01550) 720410
Fax: (01550) 720262

HIGHLY COMMENDED

Welcome to the countryside - our livestock farm overlooking the river Towy, two miles from Llandovery market town on A4069. The 17th century farmhouse is full of charm and character with inglenook fireplace, exposed stonework and beams. Spacious luxury en-suite bedrooms with bath/shower, hairdryer, TV, tea/coffee. Breathtaking views of riverside from large garden with picnic area. Ideally situated for touring Llyn Brianne Reservoir, Brecon Beacons, caves, gold mines, castles and beaches.

P		NIGHTLY B & B PER PERSON		WEEKLY D, B & B PER PERSON			3
		MIN £	MAX £	MIN £	MAX £	OPEN	3
		19.00	20.00	-	-	4 - 10	

H	Ashburnham Hotel

Ashburnham Road
Pembrey,
Llanelli SA16 0TH
Tel: (01554) 834343
Fax: (01554) 834483

HIGHLY COMMENDED

Set in landscaped grounds overlooking golf course, en-suite bedrooms with satellite television, courtesy trays. Licensed conservatory lounge bar, perfect for relaxation. Elegant restaurant with a reputation for fine cuisine. Blue Flag beach, motor racing, horse riding, golf, cycling, fishing, sailing are all close by and can be arranged.

P		NIGHTLY B & B PER PERSON		WEEKLY D, B & B PER PERSON			12
C							12
		MIN £	MAX £	MIN £	MAX £	OPEN	
		26.00	26.00	-	-	1 - 12	

FH	Glog Farm

Llangain,
Carmarthen SA33 5AY
Tel: (01267) 241271

AWARD

Glog is a small working farm, situated in a peaceful location, with views of the rolling countryside. Less than 5 miles from quiet sandy beach and castle at Llansteffan and 5 miles from Carmarthen. Within easy reach of Saundersfoot, Tenby, the West Wales coast, the Pembrokeshire Coast National Park, the Black Mountains and Gower.

P		NIGHTLY B & B PER PERSON		WEEKLY D, B & B PER PERSON			4
		MIN £	MAX £	MIN £	MAX £	OPEN	4
		20.00	20.00	180.00	180.00	1 - 12	

Prices

In this publication we go to great lengths to make sure that you have a clear, accurate idea of prices and facilities. It's all spelled out in the 'Prices' sections - and remember to confirm everything when making your booking.

Kidwelly Castle

Welcome Host

Customer care is our top priority. It's what our Welcome Host scheme is all about. Welcome Host badge or certificate holders are part of a tradition of friendliness. The Welcome Host programme, which is open to everyone from hotel staff to taxi drivers, places the emphasis on warm Welsh hospitality and first-class service.

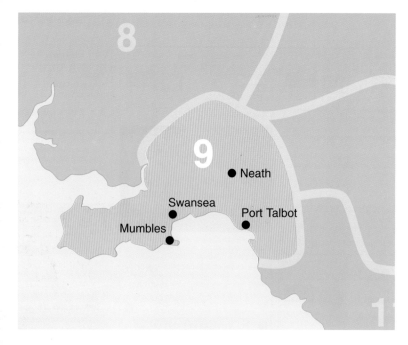

The city of Swansea enjoys a wonderful location. It stands on the grand curve of Swansea Bay at the doorstep to the beautiful Gower Peninsula and green Vale of Neath. It's a maritime city through and through – there's even a stylish Maritime Quarter complete with marina and attractive waterside developments. Modern and traditional Wales mix happily in this friendly city. At its heart is a fresh foods market where you can buy welshcakes, laverbread and cockles from Penclawdd on Gower. The pretty little sailing centre of Mumbles stands at the gateway to Gower, a lovely peninsula with a string of sandy, south-facing bays and a towering curtain of cliffs. Inland, there are the waterfalls and forests of the Afan Valley and Vale of Neath to explore.

It's a fact...

In 1956, the Gower Peninsula was the first part of Britain to be declared an 'Area of Outstanding Natural Beauty'. Swansea Museum, Wales's oldest museum, dates from the 1830s. The inaugural meeting of the Welsh Rugby Union was held at Neath in 1881. The waterwheel at the National Trust's Aberdulais Falls is Europe's largest electricity-generating waterwheel. The traditional Welsh delicacy known as laverbread (a kind of puréed seaweed) is usually eaten as an accompaniment to bacon and eggs.

La4   Mumbles

Small resort on Swansea Bay with attractive waterfront and headland pier; centre for watersports and sailing. On fringe of Gower Peninsula, a designated 'Area of Outstanding Natural Beauty'. Oystermouth Castle and Clyne Valley Country Park and Gardens nearby.

La4   Swansea

Wales's second city and gateway to the Gower Peninsula, Britain s first designated 'Area of Outstanding Natural Beauty'. Superb modern marina complex and Maritime Quarter – excellent leisure centre, with Maritime and Industrial Museum alongside. Art gallery, Tŷ Llên cultural/literature centre, Superbowl, dry ski slope and marvellous 'Plantasia' exotic plants attraction. Good shopping. Covered market with distinctively Welsh atmosphere: try the cockles, laverbread and Gower potatoes. Swansea Festival and 'Fringe' Festival in October. Theatres and cinemas, parks and gardens, restaurants and wine bars.

Swansea marina (top)

Sailing at Mumbles

Mumbles Swansea

H	Wittemberg Hotel

2 Rotherslade Road,
Langland,
Swansea SA3 4QN
Tel: (01792) 369696
Fax: (01792) 366995

COMMENDED

Informal relaxed atmosphere in this AA One Star hotel. Ample private parking. Ideal base to explore Gower - wonderful cliff walks and superb beaches, yet only five miles from Swansea. Rooms have toilet and shower en-suite, colour TV, tea/coffee making facilities. For details of weekly and short breaks or just B&B, contact resident owners Andrew and June Thomas.

		NIGHTLY B & B PER PERSON	WEEKLY D, B & B PER PERSON	🛏	11
				🛁	10
		MIN £	MAX £	MIN £	MAX £	OPEN
		22.50	27.50	149.00	205.00	2 - 12

H	Aberavon Beach Hotel

Port Talbot SA12 6QP
Tel: (01639) 884949
Fax: (01639) 897885

HIGHLY COMMENDED

Modern seafront hotel with excellent views across Swansea Bay to the Gower Peninsula, opposite a wide sandy beach. Particularly suitable for families offering exceptional value, comfortable bedrooms, elegant restaurant with fine food, new all-weather leisure centre and friendly and welcoming staff. Ideally placed 7 miles from the centre of Swansea, close to the M4 and with easy access to all the tourist attractions of South Wales and the Welsh valleys.

		NIGHTLY B & B PER PERSON	WEEKLY D, B & B PER PERSON	🛏	52
				🛁	52
		MIN £	MAX £	MIN £	MAX £	OPEN
		30.00	31.00	210.00	217.00	1 - 12

H	The Dolphin Hotel

Whitewalls,
Swansea SA1 3AB
Tel: (01792) 650011
Fax: (01792) 642871

COMMENDED

Located in a pedestrianised (but vehicle accessible) area off the city centre, the hotel is ideal for those with shopping in mind. Conversely, the Marina and beach are only five minutes walk away and there is easy access to the Gower Peninsula and other destinations of local interest. Friendly staff and attentive service assured.

		NIGHTLY B & B PER PERSON	WEEKLY D, B & B PER PERSON	🛏	66
				🛁	66
		MIN £	MAX £	MIN £	MAX £	OPEN
		22.50	37.50	240.00	500.00	1 - 12

H	The Grosvenor House Hotel

Mirador Crescent,
Uplands,
Swansea SA2 0QX
Tel: (01792) 461522
Fax: (01792) 461522

HIGHLY COMMENDED

Grosvenor House warmly welcomes businessmen and holiday visitors. Quietly situated, convenient for city centre, Mumbles and Gower. All bedrooms en-suite with colour television, clock/radio, hairdryer, trouser press, tea/coffee, fresh towels daily. Comfortable lounge, separate non-smoking dining room. Private car parking available. Colour brochure from proprietors Pat and Brian Hill. RAC Acclaimed AA QQQ.

		NIGHTLY B & B PER PERSON	WEEKLY D, B & B PER PERSON	🛏	7
				🛁	7
		MIN £	MAX £	MIN £	MAX £	OPEN
		20.00	22.00	175.00	190.00	1 - 12

H	Waters Edge Hotel

374 Mumbles Road,
Mumbles,
Swansea SA3 5TN
Tel: (01792) 401030

On the seafront within 5 minutes walking distance of the picturesque fishing village of Mumbles, also easy reach Gower Peninsula, city centre with its many attractions and Maritime Quarter. Some bedrooms and lounge with sea views, and en-suite facilities. All bedrooms have colour TV and tea/coffee facilities. Full fire certificate, licensed bar and restaurant.

		NIGHTLY B & B PER PERSON	WEEKLY D, B & B PER PERSON	🛏	7
				🛁	5
		MIN £	MAX £	MIN £	MAX £	OPEN
		16.00	20.00	196.00	210.00	1 - 12

Pets welcome

You'll see from the symbols that many places to stay welcome dogs and pets by prior arrangement. Although some sections of beach may have restrictions, there are always adjacent areas - the promenade, for example, or quieter stretches of sands - where dogs can be exercised on and sometimes off leads. Please ask at a Tourist Information Centre for advice.

Prices

Please note that all prices are PER PERSON, based on TWO PEOPLE sharing a double or twin room. SINGLE OCCUPANCY will usually be charged extra, and there may be supplements for private bath/shower. All prices include VAT. Daily rates are for bed and breakfast. Weekly rates are for dinner, B&B. Please check all prices and facilities before confirming your booking.

Cyclists and Walkers Welcome

Look out for the 'boot' and 'bike' symbols. They are displayed by places which have undertaken to provide features which cyclists and/or walkers always find welcome. These include drying facilities for wet clothes and boots, secure lockable areas for bikes, availability of packed lunches and so on. You'll even be greeted with a welcoming cup of tea or coffee on arrival!

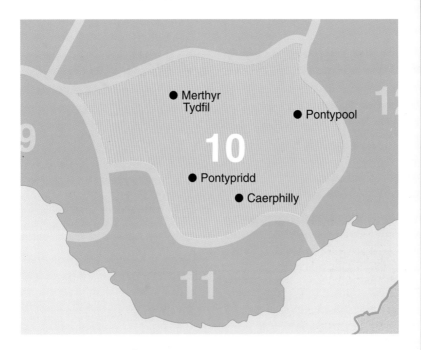

The Valleys of South Wales are full of surprises – dramatic natural beauty, country and wildlife parks, forest and cycle trails, and a huge range of attractions. Did you know that Caerphilly Castle is regarded as one of Europe's greatest surviving examples of medieval military architecture? Or that there's a scenic narrow-gauge railway which takes you into the foothills of the Brecon Beacons from Merthyr Tydfil? Or that you can enjoy everything from walking to watersports at an exceptional range of country parks? Yet the past hasn't been entirely forgotten. Although the Valleys are green again, there's a rich industrial heritage at places like the Big Pit Mining Museum, Blaenafon, and the Rhondda Heritage Park, Trehafod.

It's a fact...

Caerphilly Castle, which covers 12 hectares/30 acres, is one of Britain's largest. Its 'leaning tower' out-leans Pisa's. In the 19th century, Merthyr Tydfil was Wales's largest town and the 'iron capital of the world'. The world's first steam engine, built by Cornishman Richard Trevithick, ran from Merthyr to Abercynon in 1804. There are around 15 country parks in the Valleys. Pontypridd is singer Tom Jones's home town. Blaenafon's Big Pit Mining Museum was a working colliery until 1980. The last coalmine in the Rhondda closed at the end of 1990.

Ma4   Caerphilly   ⇌

A sight not to be missed – 13th-century Caerphilly Castle is one of Europe s finest surviving medieval strongholds and has a famous leaning tower. Golf course, shopping, good centre for exploring the Valleys and visiting Cardiff. Fine views and pleasant walks from Caerphilly Mountain. Caerphilly cheese made at the Old Court.

Mc3   Cwmbran   ⇌

A 'new town' development and administrative centre. Good leisure facilities. Llantarnam Grange Arts Centre. Shopping and sports centre with international athletics stadium. Theatre and cinemas. Well-located touring centre for the Vale of Usk and South Wales Valleys.

Le2   Merthyr Tydfil   ⇌

Once the 'iron capital of the world'. The museum in Cyfarthfa Castle, built by the Crawshay family of ironmasters and set in pleasant parkland, and the Ynysfach Heritage Centre near the town centre, tell of those times. Also visit the birthplace of hymn-writer Joseph Parry. The narrow-gauge Brecon Mountain Railway makes the most of the town's location on the doorstep of the Brecon Beacons National Park. Garwnant Forest Visitor Centre and scenic lakes in hills to the north.

Le4   Pontypridd   ⇌

Busy Valleys town which recalls its past at the Pontypridd Historical and Cultural Centre. Mining traditions are also reflected at the nearby Rhondda Heritage Park. Pontypridd is Tom Jones's home town and singers Stewart Burrows and the late Sir Geraint Evans hail from nearby Cilfynydd. John Hughes's Grogg Shop with its sculptures of famous rugby players led to worldwide fame for his unique creations.

John Hughes 'Grogg' Workshop, Pontypridd (top)

Caerphilly Castle

Caerphilly Cwmbran Merthyr Tydfil Pontypridd

WALES CYMRU
A DIFFERENT HOLIDAY EVERY DAY

Cyfarthfa Castle, Merthyr Tydfil

H	The Baverstock Hotel

Heads of the Valleys Road,
Aberdare CF44 0LX
Tel: (01685) 386221
Fax: (01685) 723670

COMMENDED

On the edge of the beautiful Brecon Beacons National Park, close to many local attractions. Comfortable licensed bar. A la carte and table d'hôte menus available. Egon Ronay recommended. Non-smoking family rooms and special weekend breaks available. The perfect base for touring south Wales. For a copy of our new brochure - Freephone 0800 716010.

	NIGHTLY B & B	WEEKLY D, B & B	🚶 50
P C	PER PERSON	PER PERSON	50
	MIN £	MAX £	MIN £	MAX £	OPEN
	22.50	40.00	185.00	285.00	1 - 12

H	Heritage Park Hotel

Coed Cae Road,
Trehafod, Porth,
Nr. Pontypridd CF37 2NP
Tel: (01443) 687057
Fax: (01443) 687060

COMMENDED ♿

Set in the heart of the Rhondda Valley, a modern but traditionally built hotel, adjacent to the Rhondda Heritage Park. The hotel also boasts a new health and leisure club, exquisitely decorated en-suite bedrooms, a fine restaurant and a warm Welsh welcome.

	NIGHTLY B & B	WEEKLY D, B & B	44
P	PER PERSON	PER PERSON	44
	MIN £	MAX £	MIN £	MAX £	OPEN
	28.97	33.97	272.79	307.79	1 - 12

H	Griffin Hotel

Rudry,
Caerphilly CF83 3EA
Tel: (01222) 869735
Fax: (01222) 863681

HIGHLY COMMENDED

A courtyard hotel standing in open countryside above Caerphilly. All bedrooms have en-suite facilities and the restaurant offers a wide choice of food and wine. Situated 15 minutes from the M4, an ideal centre for sightseeing, walking, golf and horse riding.

	NIGHTLY B & B	WEEKLY D, B & B	30
P C	PER PERSON	PER PERSON	30
	MIN £	MAX £	MIN £	MAX £	OPEN
	20.00	25.00	–	–	1 - 12

GH	Springfields Guest House

371 Llantarnam Road,
Llantarnam,
Cwmbran NP44 3BN
Tel: (016633) 482509

COMMENDED

Family run for 24 years. Situated 3 miles from M4 off the A4042 at Llantarnam - a semi-rural location. Comfort and care are our main concern. We have enjoyed Springfields and so have our customers. Ideal for touring, close to Caerleon, Big Pit, Cardiff, Wye Valley. Thank you. Joan, Graham and Theresa.

	NIGHTLY B & B	WEEKLY D, B & B	9
P	PER PERSON	PER PERSON	6
	MIN £	MAX £	MIN £	MAX £	OPEN
	16.50	19..00	–	–	1 - 12

Wales: Castles and Historic Places

- **Beautifully produced full-colour guide to more than 140 historic sites**
- **Castles, abbeys, country houses, prehistoric and Roman remains**
- **Detailed maps**

£7.25 inc. p&p

(see 'Get Yourself a Guide' at the end of the book)

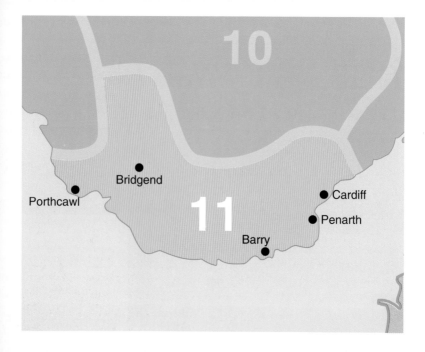

Bridgend

Porthcawl

10

11

Cardiff

Penarth

Barry

Cardiff is Wales's cosmopolitan capital city. It's a place of culture and the arts, with fine museums and theatres. It's also a city of great style – Cardiff's neoclassical civic architecture has won praise worldwide while the lavish city-centre castle, a seriously Victorian creation, never fails to astonish. The castle was built with the wealth generated by Cardiff's booming 19th-century seaport. The city is now renewing its maritime links through the exciting Cardiff Bay development, which is transforming the old waterfront. Close to the city there's attractive coast and countryside. The pastoral Vale of Glamorgan is dotted with picturesque villages and thatched cottages. And along the shore there's everything from the spectacular cliffs of the Glamorgan Heritage Coast to the popular resorts of Barry Island and Porthcawl.

It's a fact…

Cardiff was declared capital city of Wales in 1955. The Cardiff Bay development will create 8 miles of new waterfront and a 202-hectare/ 500-acre freshwater lake. In 1999 Cardiff plays host to the Rugby World Cup. Cardiff-born author Roald Dahl was baptised in the city's Norwegian Church. The Glamorgan Heritage Coast, designated in 1973, runs for 14 miles between Aberthaw and Porthcawl. Merthyr Mawr has the highest sand dunes in Britain, rising to over 61m/200ft. Ewenny, near Bridgend, boasts Wales's oldest working pottery.

Mb5   Cardiff   ⇌

Capital of Wales, business, trade and entertainment centre. Splendid Civic Centre, lovely parkland, modern pedestrianised shopping centre, new waterfront development, good restaurants, theatres, cinemas, clubs and sports facilities, including ice-rink and Superbowl. Visit St David's Hall for top-class entertainment. Ornate city-centre castle. National Museum and Gallery has a fine collection of Impressionist paintings. Industrial and Maritime Museum and Techniquest science discovery centre on Cardiff Bay waterfront. National Stadium is home of Welsh rugby. Llandaff Cathedral close by as well as fascinating collection of old farmhouses and other buildings at the Museum of Welsh Life, St Fagans.

St Fagans Castle, Museum of Welsh Life

The Pierhead Building, Cardiff Bay (top)

Cardiff

H	The Angel Hotel

Castle Street,
Cardiff CF1 2QZ
Tel: (01222) 232633
Fax: (01222) 396212

HIGHLY COMMENDED

Beautiful four star Victorian hotel, situated in the heart of city centre overlooking Cardiff Castle and near all main shopping arcades and local attractions. 103 luxurious en-suite bedrooms, some with castle views, health suite with sauna and solarium, free car parking. Relax in the cocktail bar before dining in our elegant restaurant. *i*

P, C, ✂, ❍	NIGHTLY B & B PER PERSON	WEEKLY D, B & B PER PERSON	🚪 103 🛏 103
	MIN £	MAX £	MIN £	MAX £	OPEN
	36.00	51.25	POA	POA	1 - 12

H	Austins Hotel

11 Coldstream Terrace,
City Centre,
Cardiff CF1 8LJ
Tel: (01222) 377148

COMMENDED

Small friendly family run hotel 300 metres from Cardiff Castle overlooking the river Taff. All city centre attractions are within a few minutes walk. Cardiff Central station is 10 minutes walk along the river. All rooms have tea/coffee and colour TV. En-suite rooms available. A warm welcome offered to all nationalities. Come, enjoy Cardiff this year. *i*

❍, C, ✂, ▥	NIGHTLY B & B PER PERSON	WEEKLY D, B & B PER PERSON	🚪 11 🛏 3
	MIN £	MAX £	MIN £	MAX £	OPEN
	15.00	17.50	–	–	1 - 12

H	Clare Court Hotel

46-48 Clare Road,
Cardiff CF1 7RS
Tel: (01222) 344839
Fax: (01222) 665856

APPROVED

Family run hotel 5-10 minutes walk to bus, railway stations, city centre, walking distance to castle, football, rugby and cricket grounds, sport and athletic stadiums. All rooms with en-suite bath/shower, colour TV, radio, telephone, tea/coffee machines. Licensed bar, restaurant. *i*

❍, ▥, ❍❍	NIGHTLY B & B PER PERSON	WEEKLY D, B & B PER PERSON	🚪 8 🛏 8
	MIN £	MAX £	MIN £	MAX £	OPEN
	16.00	18.00	147.00	–	1 - 12

Cyclists and Walkers Welcome

Look out for the 'boot' and 'bike' symbols. They are displayed by places which have undertaken to provide features which cyclists and/or walkers always find welcome. These include drying facilities for wet clothes and boots, secure lockable areas for bikes, availability of packed lunches and so on. You'll even be greeted with a welcoming cup of tea or coffee on arrival!

Cardiff Castle's magnificent Library

Cardiff

Cardiff City Hall

H	Wynford Hotel

Clare Street,
Cardiff CF1 8SD
Tel: (01222) 371983
Fax: (01222) 340477

Very close to the city centre, train and bus stations, the Wynford is a privately owned hotel, personally supervised by the proprietor, and priding itself on a warm welcome, attentive service and excellent facilities. Comfortable lounge, two cosy bars, occasional music and dancing, bistro and restaurant. All rooms have colour TV, telephone, and many have private bathroom. French, Spanish and German spoken. Night porter. Video linked security car park.

		NIGHTLY B & B PER PERSON		WEEKLY D, B & B PER PERSON			20
							16
		MIN £	MAX £	MIN £	MAX £	OPEN	
		19.00	26.00	-	-	1 - 12	

H	Egerton Grey Country House Hotel

Porthkerry,
Nr. Cardiff CF62 3BZ
Tel: (01446) 711666
Fax: (01446) 711690

HIGHLY COMMENDED

Luxurious former rectory, ten miles west of Cardiff in a beautiful green valley facing the coast. Superb comfort and cuisine. Former "County Hotel and Restaurant of the Year" in various prestigious guides. Inexpensive short breaks all year round. Ideal base for exploring Cardiff, Gower Peninsula and Brecon Beacons National Park.

		NIGHTLY B & B PER PERSON		WEEKLY D, B & B PER PERSON			10
							10
		MIN £	MAX £	MIN £	MAX £	OPEN	
		37.50	60.00	295.00	375.00	1 - 12	

H	Miskin Manor

Pendoylan Road,
Groes Faen,
Pontyclun CF72 8ND
Tel: (01443) 224204
Fax: (01443) 237606

HIGHLY COMMENDED

Charming country house hotel with award winning restaurant, set in 20 acres close to Cardiff near Junction 34 M4. Large spacious rooms and lounges. Leisure facilities on site including swimming, squash, gym, sunbeds, sauna, spa, snooker. Golf and riding nearby. All bedrooms en-suite, two four posters and Prince of Wales suite.

		NIGHTLY B & B PER PERSON		WEEKLY D, B & B PER PERSON			32
							32
		MIN £	MAX £	MIN £	MAX £	OPEN	
		50.00	87.50	-	-	1 - 12	

GH	Sant-y-Nyll

St Brides-Super-Ely CF5 6EZ
Tel: (01446) 760209
Fax: (01446) 760209

HIGHLY COMMENDED

Well appointed beautiful Georgian country house standing in own grounds with spectacular views over Vale of Glamorgan. Close to centre of Cardiff but still in heart of country - Museum of Welsh Life two miles - restaurants within walking distance. Monika and Paul Renwick are waiting to welcome you.

		NIGHTLY B & B PER PERSON		WEEKLY D, B & B PER PERSON			6
							1
		MIN £	MAX £	MIN £	MAX £	OPEN	
		17.50	35.00	150.00	195.00	1 - 12	

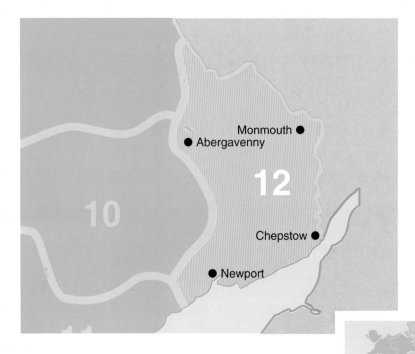

These two lovely valleys, close to the border, serve as the best possible introduction to Wales. The thickly wooded Wye Valley snakes its way northwards from Chepstow through countryside which is beautiful in all seasons. It's a walker's paradise, with a wonderful choice of trails including woodland, riverside and Offa's Dyke paths. Rolling green hills separate the Wye from the Usk, another beautiful river valley which reaches the sea at Newport.

Fishermen, as well as walkers, love this part of Wales, for both rivers are famed for their salmon and trout. These borderlands, a natural gateway into Wales over the centuries, are dotted with historic sites of great significance – the Roman town of Caerleon, castles at almost every turn, and the splendid 17th-century mansion of Tredegar House, Newport.

It's a fact...

The Wye Valley between Chepstow and Monmouth is an 'Area of Outstanding Natural Beauty', designated in 1971. Among the Wye Valley's earliest tourists was poet William Wordsworth, inspired to write *'Lines Composed a Few Miles Above Tintern Abbey'* in 1798. Britain's first stone-built castle was constructed at Chepstow in 1067. Charles Stewart Rolls, of Rolls-Royce celebrity, is a famous son of Monmouth – his statue stands in the town square. The Skirrid Inn at Llanfihangel Crucorney near Abergavenny is reputed to be the oldest pub in Wales.

Mc1   Abergavenny   🚉

Flourishing market town with backdrop of mountains at south-eastern gateway to Brecon Beacons National Park. Pony trekking in nearby Black Mountains. Castle, Museum of Childhood and Home. Leisure centre. Monmouthshire and Brecon Canal runs just to the west of the town. Excellent touring base for the lovely Vale of Usk and Brecon Beacons.

Me1   Monmouth

Historic market town in picturesque Wye Valley – birthplace of Henry V and Charles Rolls (of Rolls-Royce). Interesting local history museum with collection of Nelson memorabilia. Rare fortified gateway still spans the River Monnow. Ruined castle close to town centre. Well located for touring Wye Valley and borderland Wales.

Me3   Chepstow   🚉

Attractive hilly town with substantial remains of a great stone castle – reputedly the first to be built in Britain – above the Wye. Fortified gate still stands in main street and medieval walls remain. Good shopping. Museum, Stuart Crystal Engraving Workshop. Sunday market, fine racecourse, excellent walks – beginning of the Wye Valley Walk and Offa's Dyke Path. Ideal for touring beautiful Wye Valley.

Md3   Usk

Ancient borough on River Usk; excellent salmon fishing and inns. Good walks. Rural Life Museum, grass skiing. Great castle of Raglan 5 miles north. Sailing and other watersports on nearby Llandegfedd Reservoir. Good central location for sightseeing.

Mc3   Cwmbran   🚉

A 'new town' – development and administrative centre. Good leisure facilities. Llantarnam Grange Arts Centre. Shopping and sports centre with international athletics stadium. Theatre and cinemas. Well-located touring centre for the Vale of Usk and South Wales Valleys.

Usk

The River Wye at Llandogo (top)

Abergavenny Chepstow Cwmbran Monmouth

GH	Park Guest House

36 Hereford Road,
Abergavenny NP7 5RA
Tel: (01873) 853715

COMMENDED

Attractive detached georgian guest house, close to town centre. All rooms with hand basin, beverage tray, TV and radio. Two bathrooms, lounge, dining room with separate tables. High quality four course evening meals available by arrangement. Fully licensed. Free private parking. Convenient for Brecon Beacons, Big Pit, castles and museums. Detailed brochure available on request.

i

P 🛁 C ✂ 🏧 🍽	NIGHTLY B & B PER PERSON	WEEKLY D, B & B PER PERSON	🛏 7 🛁 -
	MIN £ 16.00	MAX £ 18.00	MIN £ 180.00	MAX £ 195.00	OPEN 1 - 12

Pets welcome

You'll see from the symbols that many places to stay welcome dogs and pets by prior arrangement. Although some sections of beach may have restrictions, there are always adjacent areas - the promenade, for example, or quieter stretches of sands - where dogs can be exercised on and sometimes off leads. Please ask at a Tourist Information Centre for advice.

A Journey Through Wales

- **Magnificently produced book**, the ideal gift or memento
- **High quality photographs** with accompanying text take you on a tour of Wales
- **Classic views** of Wales's scenic mountains and coastline
- **A complete pictorial record** - everything from powerful castles to colourful craft workshops, picturesque villages to narrow-gauge railways

£5.10 inc. p&p
(see 'Get Yourself a Guide' at the end of the book)

FH	High House Farm

Bryngwyn,
Raglan NP5 2BS
Tel: (01291) 690529

HIGHLY COMMENDED

Traditional Welsh farmhouse built around 1640 with dairy and beef enterprises. Comfortable rooms with tea/coffee facilities. A guests' lounge enjoys extensive views towards the Sugar Loaf and Black Mountains.

i

P 🏧	NIGHTLY B & B PER PERSON	WEEKLY D, B & B PER PERSON	🛏 3 🛁 1
	MIN £ 18.00	MAX £ 18.00	MIN £ -	MAX £ -	OPEN 4 - 10

FGH	Penylan Farm

St. Brides Netherwent,
Magor,
Newport
Tel: (01633) 400267

COMMENDED

Splendid Elizabethan farmhouse with oak beams, Inglenook fire places, on hilltop overlooking beautiful St. Brides valley. Quiet rural setting. 2 miles M4 and Wentwood Forest. Many golf courses including St. Pierre, Celtic Manor, castles, excellent eating places - all within 20 minutes drive. Good overnight stop for Irish Ferries. Welsh hospitality assured.

i

P ✂ 🏧 🍽	C	NIGHTLY B & B PER PERSON	WEEKLY D, B & B PER PERSON	🛏 2 🛁 1
		MIN £ 20.00	MAX £ 24.00	MIN £ -	MAX £ -	OPEN 4 - 11

H	The Parkway Hotel

Cwmbran Drive,
Cwmbran NP44 3UW
Tel: (01633) 871199
Fax: (01633) 869160

HIGHLY COMMENDED

The Parkway is a 4 star luxury hotel situated in 7.5 acre grounds. Facilities include 70 en-suite bedrooms and 'The Colonial Club' health and leisure complex. Close to Cardiff, Brecon Beacons, Big Pit Mining Museum and Museum of Welsh Life, St Fagans.

P C ✂ 🏧 🍽	🏧	NIGHTLY B & B PER PERSON	WEEKLY D, B & B PER PERSON	🛏 70 🛁 70
		MIN £ 45.88	MAX £ 52.71	MIN £ 348.49	MAX £ 348.49	OPEN 1 - 12

H	Wyndham Arms

Clearwell,
Nr. Coleford GL16 8JT
Tel: (01594) 833666
Fax: (01594) 836450

 HIGHLY COMMENDED

14th century village inn, now a fine 17 bedroomed hotel with award winning restaurant. In the Stanford family's competent management since 1973. The ideal place to stay for seeing the Wye Valley and the Royal Forest of Dean. On Sundays you can stay free provided you have two restaurant dinners. Children and dogs welcome.

P C ✂ 🏧 🍽	🏧	NIGHTLY B & B PER PERSON	WEEKLY D, B & B PER PERSON	🛏 17 🛁 17
		MIN £ 30.50	MAX £ 32.50	MIN £ 280.00	MAX £ 280.00	OPEN 1 - 12

WALES ❧ CYMRU
A DIFFERENT HOLIDAY EVERY DAY

GH | Church Farm Guest House

Mitchel Troy,
Monmouth NP5 4HZ
Tel: (01600) 712176

COMMENDED

A spacious and homely 16th century former farmhouse with oak beams and inglenook fireplaces. Set in large attractive garden with stream. Easy access to A40 and only two miles from historic Monmouth. Excellent base for Wye Valley, Forest of Dean and Black Mountains. Large car park, terrace, barbecue, colour TV, central heating, tea/coffee making facilities.

i

		NIGHTLY B & B PER PERSON		WEEKLY D, B & B PER PERSON		⏅ 8
						⏅ 6
		MIN £	MAX £	MIN £	MAX £	OPEN
		17.00	20.00	189.00	210.00	1 - 12

FH | New House Farm

Dingestow,
Nr Monmouth NP5 4EB
Tel: (01600) 740245
Fax: (01600) 740245

COMMENDED

New House Farm is a 300 acre working farm set in peaceful countryside with magnificent views. Ideally situated for touring Wye Valley, Brecon Beacons and Forest of Dean. A warm welcome awaits you with a high standard of comfort and cooking. Children are welcome with animals to see. Circular walks start on the farm.

i

		NIGHTLY B & B PER PERSON		WEEKLY D, B & B PER PERSON		⏅ 3
						⏅ -
		MIN £	MAX £	MIN £	MAX £	OPEN
		17.00	19.00	-	-	1 - 12

H | Greyhound Inn/Hotel

Llantrisant,
Nr. Usk NP5 1LE
Tel: (01291) 672505
Fax: (01291) 673255
Central Res: (01291) 673447

COMMENDED

The 17th century Greyhound Inn offers excellent home cooked meals, real ales and fine wines. Accommodation in the stone barns is of the highest standards with all modern day comforts. Shop in our Country Pine and Antiques showroom. Situated in beautiful Vale of Usk. Wales's ideal holiday base!

i

		NIGHTLY B & B PER PERSON		WEEKLY D, B & B PER PERSON		⏅ 10
						⏅ 10
		MIN £	MAX £	MIN £	MAX £	OPEN
		25.00	28.00	POA	POA	1 - 12

H | The Rat Trap Hotel

Llangeview,
Chepstow Road,
Nr. Usk NP5 1EY
Tel: (01291) 673288
Fax: (01291) 673305

HIGHLY COMMENDED

One mile from the picturesque town of Usk, the locality provides a perfect base from which all of Gwent's fine historical attractions can be explored - Caerleon, Wye Valley and many more. Our brasserie is renowned for the fine quality of our fresh food and the excellent wine list.

i

		NIGHTLY B & B PER PERSON		WEEKLY D, B & B PER PERSON		⏅ 13
						⏅ 13
		MIN £	MAX £	MIN £	MAX £	OPEN
		24.50	29.50	-	-	1 - 12

The Monmouthshire and Brecon Canal at Talybont on Usk

Make the most of your stay in Wales by contacting one of our Tourist Information Centres for help on all aspects of your holiday. TIC staff will be delighted to assist with:
● booking your accommodation *(see below)* ● places to visit ● places to eat ● things to do
● routes to take ● national and local events ● maps, guides and books

Tourist Information Centres

Normal opening times are 10am–5.30pm. These hours may vary to suit local circumstances. Those marked with an asterisk (*) are open seasonally only (April–September).

The Bed Booking Service is free for local reservations. A £1.00 fee applies to bookings made further afield in Wales.

Aberaeron	The Quay, Aberaeron SA46 0BT	Tel: (01545) 570602
Aberdovey / Aberdyfi *	Wharf Gardens, Aberdovey LL35 0ED	Tel: (01654) 767321
Abergavenny	Swan Meadow, Monmouth Road, Abergavenny NP7 5HH	Tel: (01873) 857588
Aberystwyth	Terrace Road, Aberystwyth SY23 2AG	Tel: (01970) 612125
Bala	Penllyn, Pensarn Road, Bala LL23 7SR	Tel: (01678) 521021
Bangor *	Little Chef Services, A55/A5 Llandegai, Bangor LL57 7BG	Tel: (01248) 352786
Barmouth *	Old Library, Station Road, Barmouth LL42 1LU	Tel: (01341) 280787
Barry Island *	The Triangle, Paget Road, Barry Island CF62 5TQ	Tel: (01446) 747171
Betws-y-Coed	Royal Oak Stables, Betws-y-Coed LL24 0AH	Tel: (01690) 710426
Blaenau Ffestiniog *	Isallt, High Street, Blaenau Ffestiniog LL41 3HD	Tel: (01766) 830360
Borth *	Cambrian Terrace, Borth SY24 5HU	Tel: (01970) 871174
Brecon	Cattle Market Car Park, Brecon LD3 9DA	Tel: (01874) 622485
Builth Wells *	Groe Car Park, Builth Wells LD2 3BT	Tel: (01982) 553307
Caerleon *	5 High Street, Caerleon NP6 1AG	Tel: (01633) 422656
Caernarfon	Oriel Pendeitsh, Castle Street, Caernarfon LL55 2NA	Tel: (01286) 672232
Caerphilly	Twyn Square, Caerphilly CF83 1XX	Tel: (01222) 880011
Cardiff	Central Station, Cardiff CF1 1QY	Tel: (01222) 227281
Cardigan	Theatr Mwldan, Bath House Road, Cardigan SA43 2JY	Tel: (01239) 613230
Carmarthen	Lammas Street, Carmarthen SA31 3AQ	Tel: (01267) 231557
Chepstow	Castle Car Park, Bridge Street, Chepstow NP6 5EY	Tel: (01291) 623772
Colwyn Bay	40 Station Road, Colwyn Bay LL29 8BU	Tel: (01492) 530478
Conwy	Conwy Castle Visitor Centre, Conwy LL32 8LD	Tel: (01492) 592248
Corris *	Craft Centre, Corris, nr Machynlleth SY20 9SP	Tel: (01654) 761244
Crickhowell *	Beaufort Chambers, Beaufort Street, Crickhowell NP8 1AA	Tel: (01873) 812105
Cwmcarn *	Visitor Centre, Cwmcarn Forest Drive, nr Cross Keys NP1 7FA	Tel: (01495) 272001
Dolgellau	Tŷ Meirion, Eldon Square, Dolgellau LL40 1PU	Tel: (01341) 422888
Elan Valley *	Elan Valley Visitor Centre, Elan Valley, nr Rhayader LD6 5HP	Tel: (01597) 810898
Ewloe *	Autolodge Services, A55 Westbound, Northophall, Ewloe CH7 6HE	Tel: (01244) 541597
Fishguard Harbour *	Passenger Concourse, The Harbour, Goodwick, Fishguard SA64 0BU	Tel: (01348) 872037
Fishguard Town	4 Hamilton Street, Fishguard SA65 9HL	Tel: (01348) 873484
Harlech *	Gwyddfor House, High Street, Harlech LL46 2YA	Tel: (01766) 780658
Haverfordwest	Old Bridge, Haverfordwest SA61 2EZ	Tel: (01437) 763110
Holyhead	The Kiosk, Stena Line, Terminal 1, Holyhead LL65 1DR	Tel: (01407) 762622
Kilgetty *	Kingsmoor Common, Kilgetty SA68 0YA	Tel: (01834) 813672
Knighton	Offa's Dyke Centre, West Street, Knighton LD7 1EW	Tel: (01547) 528753
Lake Vyrnwy *	Unit 2, Vyrnwy Craft Workshops, Lake Vyrnwy SY10 0LY	Tel: (01691) 870346
Llanberis *	41a High Street, Llanberis	Tel: (01286) 870765
Llanberis *	41a High Street, Llanberis	Tel: (01286) 870765
Llandeilo *	Car Park, Crescent Road, Llandeilo	Tel: (01558) 824226

Llandovery *	King's Road, Llandovery SA20 0AW	Tel: (01550) 720693
Llandrindod Wells	Old Town Hall, Memorial Gardens, Llandrindod Wells LD1 5DL	Tel: (01597) 822600
Llandudno	1-2 Chapel Street, Llandudno LL30 2YU	Tel: (01492) 876413
Llanelli	Public Library, Vaughan Street, Llanelli SA15 3AS	Tel: (01554) 772020
Llanfairpwllgwyngyll	Station Site, Llanfairpwllgwyngyll LL61 5UJ	Tel: (01248) 713177
Llangollen	Town Hall, Castle Street, Llangollen LL20 5PD	Tel: (01978) 860828
Llanidloes	Town Hall, Great Oak Street, Llanidloes SY18 6BN	Tel: (01686) 412605
Llanwrtyd Wells *	Tŷ Barcud, The Square, Llanwrtyd Wells LD5 4RB	Tel: (01591) 610666
Machynlleth	Canolfan Owain Glyndŵr, Machynlleth SY20 8EE	Tel: (01654) 702401
Magor	First Services and Lodge, Junction 23a M4, Magor NP6 3YL	Tel: (01633) 881122
Merthyr Tydfil	14a Glebeland Street, Merthyr Tydfil CF47 8AU	Tel: (01685) 379884
Milford Haven *	94 Charles Street, Milford Haven SA73 2HL	Tel: (01646) 690866
Mold *	Library, Museum and Art Gallery, Earl Road, Mold CH7 1AP	Tel: (01352) 759331
Monmouth *	Shire Hall, Agincourt Square, Monmouth NP5 3DY	Tel: (01600) 713899
Mumbles *	Oystermouth Square, Mumbles, Swansea SA3 4DQ	Tel: (01792) 361302
Narberth	Town Hall, Narberth SA67 7AR	Tel: (01834) 860061
New Quay *	Church Street, New Quay SA45 9NZ	Tel: (01545) 560865
Newcastle Emlyn *	Market Hall, Newcastle Emlyn SA38 9AE	Tel: (01239) 711333
Newport	Newport Museum & Art Gallery, John Frost Square, Newport NP9 1HZ	Tel: (01633) 842962
Newtown	Central Car Park, Newtown SY16 2PW	Tel: (01686) 625580
Pembroke *	Visitor Centre, Commons Road, Pembroke SA71 4EA	Tel: (01646) 622388
Pembroke Dock *	The Guntower, Front Street, Pembroke Dock SA72 6JZ	Tel: (01646) 622246
Penarth *	Penarth Pier, The Esplanade, Penarth CF64 3AU	Tel: (01222) 708849
Pont Abraham	Pont Abraham Services, Junction 49 M4, Llanedi SA4 1FP	Tel: (01792) 883838
Pontneddfechan *	nr Glyn Neath SA11 5NR	Tel: (01639) 721795
Pontypridd	Historical and Cultural Centre, The Old Bridge, Pontypridd CF37 3PE	Tel: (01443) 409512
Porthcawl *	Old Police Station, John Street, Porthcawl CF36 3DT	Tel: (01656) 786639
Porthmadog	High Street, Porthmadog LL49 9LP	Tel: (01766) 512981
Prestatyn *	Scala Cinema, High Street, Prestatyn LL19 9LH	Tel: (01745) 889092
Presteigne *	Victoria House, 52 High Street, Presteigne LD8 2BE	Tel: (01544) 260193
Pwllheli	Min y Don, Station Square, Pwllheli LL53 5HG	Tel: (01758) 613000
Rhayader *	Leisure Centre, Rhayader LD6 5BU	Tel: (01597) 810591
Rhos on Sea *	The Promenade, Rhos on Sea LL28 4EP	Tel: (01492) 548778
Rhyl	Rhyl Children's Village, West Parade, Rhyl LL18 1HZ	Tel: (01745) 355068
Ruthin	Ruthin Craft Centre, Park Road, Ruthin LL15 1BB	Tel: (01824) 703992
St David's	City Hall, St David's SA62 6SD	Tel: (01437) 720392
Sarn	Sarn Park Services, Junction 36 M4, nr Bridgend CF32 9SY	Tel: (01656) 654906
Swansea	PO Box 59, Singleton Street, Swansea SA1 3QG	Tel: (01792) 468321
Tenby	The Croft, Tenby SA70 8AP	Tel: (01834) 842402
Tregaron *	The Square, Tregaron SY25 6JN	Tel: (01974) 298144
Tywyn *	High Street, Tywyn LL36 9AD	Tel: (01654) 710070
Welshpool	Flash Leisure Centre, Salop Road, Welshpool SY21 7DH	Tel: (01938) 552043
Wrexham	Lambpit Street, Wrexham LL11 1WN	Tel: (01978) 292015

And at Oswestry on the Wales/England border

Heritage Centre	2 Church Terrace, Oswestry SY11 2TE	Tel: (01691) 662753
Mile End Services	Oswestry SY11 4JA	Tel: (01691) 662488

Wales in London's West End

If you're in London, call in at the Wales Information Bureau, British Travel Centre, 12 Lower Regent Street, Piccadilly Circus, London SW1Y 4PQ. Tel (0171) 409 0969. Staff there will give you all the information you need to plan your visit to Wales.

81

Further Information

Travel facts

Rail Information

For all enquiries please telephone (01345) 484950, or contact your local travel agent or principal station.

Wales's Narrow-Gauge Railways

There are eight members of Wales's narrow-gauge 'Great Little Trains': Bala Lake Railway, Brecon Mountain Railway (Merthyr Tydfil), Ffestiniog Railway (Porthmadog), Llanberis Lake Railway, Talyllyn Railway (Tywyn), Vale of Rheidol Railway (Aberystwyth), Welsh Highland Railway (Porthmadog) and Welshpool and Llanfair Railway (Llanfair Caereinion). Details are available from The Great Little Trains of Wales, FREEPOST, The Station, Llanfair Caereinion SY21 0SF (Tel: 01938-810441).

The railways operating independently of 'Great Little Trains' are: Fairbourne and Barmouth Steam Railway (Tel: 01341-250362), Gwili Railway, nr Carmarthen (Tel: 01267-230666), Llangollen Railway (Tel: 01978-860951), Snowdon Mountain Railway, Llanberis (Tel: 01286-870223) and Teifi Valley Railway, nr Newcastle Emlyn (Tel: 01559-371077).

Coach Information

Contact your local travel agent or National Express office. For further information and all National Express credit/debit card bookings please telephone (0990) 808080. For details of your nearest National Express agent please telephone: (0990) 010104 (calls cost a maximum of 10p per minute, less at off-peak times).

Travel Hotline - (0891) 910910

One call covers it all. Phone this number for information on all of Britain's train, express coach and rural bus services - and you can also make credit card bookings at the same time. The hotline is open 6am-9pm seven days a week (calls cost 49p per minute peak times, 39p per minute at all other times).

By sea

Five services operate across the Irish Sea:

Cork to Swansea
Swansea-Cork Ferries. Tel: (01792) 456116.

Dublin to Holyhead
Irish Ferries.
General Enquiries Tel: (0990) 171717.
Firm Bookings Tel: (0345) 171717.

Dun Laoghaire to Holyhead
Stena Line – a choice of three services: High-Speed Superferry, Sea Lynx Catamaran and Ferry. Tel: (0990) 707070.

Rosslare to Fishguard
Stena Line – a choice of two services: Sea Lynx Catamaran and Ferry. Tel: (0990) 707070.

Rosslare to Pembroke
Irish Ferries.
General Enquiries Tel: (0990) 171717.
Firm Bookings Tel: (0345) 171717.

By air

There are direct flights from Aberdeen, Amsterdam, Belfast, Brussels, Channel Islands, Dublin, Edinburgh, Glasgow, Isle of Man, Manchester and Paris to Cardiff International Airport (Tel: 01446-711111), 12 miles from the city centre. There are many worldwide connections to Cardiff via most of these airports. Manchester and Birmingham Airports are also convenient gateways for Wales.

The following organisations and authorities will be pleased to provide any further information you require when planning your holiday to Wales.

Wales Tourist Board, Dept HGF, Davis Street, Cardiff CF1 2FU Tel: (01222) 475226

Holiday information is also available from:

North Wales Tourism, Dept HGF, 77 Conway Road, Colwyn Bay LL29 7BL Tel: (01492) 531731 Holiday Bookings (0800) 834820

Mid Wales Tourism, Dept HGF, The Station, Machynlleth SY20 8TG Tel: (01654) 702653 Holiday Bookings: (0800) 273747

Tourism South and West Wales, Dept HGF, Charter Court, Enterprise Park, Swansea SA7 9DB Tel: (01792) 781212 (quote Dept HGF) Holiday Bookings: (0800) 243731

Tourism South and West Wales, Dept HGF, Old Bridge, Haverfordwest, Pembrokeshire SA61 2EZ Tel: (01437) 766388 (quote Dept HGF) Holiday Bookings: (0800) 243731

Wales on the Internet

A wide range of travel and holiday information on Wales is now available on the Wales Tourist Board's Internet address:
www.tourism.wales.gov.uk

Gwyliau Cymru/ Festivals of Wales

This is the collective voice for over 50 arts festivals, embracing everything from classical music to jazz, children's events to drama.
For more information, please contact:
Festivals of Wales, Red House, Newtown SY16 3LE. Tel: (01686) 626442

Other useful addresses

Brecon Beacons National Park,
Park Office, 7 Glamorgan Street,
Brecon LD3 7DP
Tel: (01874) 624437

Cadw: Welsh Historic
Monuments,
Crown Building, Cathays Park,
Cardiff CF1 3NQ
Tel: (01222) 500200

Football Association of Wales,
3 Westgate Street, Cardiff CF1 1DD
Tel: (01222) 372325

Forestry Enterprise (Forestry
Commission),
Victoria House, Victoria Terrace,
Aberystwyth SY23 2DQ
Tel: (01970) 612367

National Trust,
North Wales Regional Office,
Trinity Square,
Llandudno LL30 2DE
Tel: (01492) 860123

National Trust,
South Wales Regional Office,
The King's Head, Bridge Street,
Llandeilo SA19 6BB
Tel: (01558) 822800

National Rivers Authority,
(Fisheries and Conservation
enquiries), Plas-yr-Afon,
St Mellons Business Park,
St Mellons, Cardiff CF3 0LT
Tel: (01222) 770088

Offa's Dyke Centre,
West Street, Knighton LD7 1EN
Tel: (01547) 528753

Pembrokeshire Coast National
Park,
National Park Department,
County Offices, St Thomas Green,
Haverfordwest SA61 1QZ
Tel: (01437) 764591

Ramblers' Association in Wales,
Ty'r Cerddwyr, High Street,
Gresford, Wrexham LL12 8PT
Tel: (01978) 855148

Snowdonia National Park,
Snowdonia National Park Office,
Penrhyndeudraeth LL48 6LS
Tel: (01766) 770274

Surfcall Wales
(daily surf/weather conditions at
all major beaches)
Tel: (0839) 505697/360361
Calls cost 39p per minute cheap
rate, 49p per minute at all other
times

Taste of Wales-*Blas ar Gymru*,
Welsh Food Promotions Ltd,
Cardiff Business Technology
Centre, Senghenydd Road,
Cardiff CF2 4AY
Tel: (01222) 640456

Wales Craft Council,
Park Lane House, 7 High Street,
Welshpool SY21 7JP
Tel: (01938) 555313

Welsh Golfing Union,
Catsafh, Newport NP6 1JQ
Tel: (01633) 430830

Welsh Rugby Union,
Cardiff Arms Park, PO Box 22,
Cardiff CF1 1JL
Tel: (01222) 390111

Youth Hostels Association,
1 Cathedral Road,
Cardiff CF1 9HA
Tel: (01222) 396766

**Trespass – a word of
warning**

If you're out and about
enjoying an activity holiday –
walking off established
footpaths, mountain biking, or
even landing your paraglider! –
please obtain permission from
landowners. To avoid any
problems, it's always best to
seek out the appropriate
permission beforehand.

Information for visitors with disabilities

Discovering Accessible Wales is an
information-packed guide for
visitors who may have impaired
movement or are confined to a
wheelchair. The book is available
free from the Wales Tourist Board.
See 'Guides and Maps' at the end
of this publication for details.

For details of other wheelchair-
accessible accommodation
inspected to the same standards
please contact the Holiday Care
Service. This organisation also
provides a wide range of other
travel and holiday information
for disabled visitors:

Holiday Care Service,
2nd Floor, Imperial Buildings,
Victoria Road, Horley,
Surrey RH6 7PZ
Tel: (01293) 774535

Other helpful organisations

Wales Council for the Blind,
Shand House, 20 Newport Road,
Cardiff CF2 1DB
Tel: (01222) 473954

Wales Council for the Deaf,
Maritime Offices,
Woodland Terrace, Maes-y-Coed,
Pontypridd CF37 1DZ
Tel: (01443) 485687
Minicom: (01443) 485686

Disability Wales,
Llys Ifor, Crescent Road,
Caerphilly CF83 1XL
Tel: (01222) 887325/6/7/8

British Tourist Authority Overseas Offices

Your enquiries will be welcome at the offices of the British Tourist Authority in the following countries:

ARGENTINA
BTA, 2nd Floor,
Avenida Cordoba 645,
1054 Buenos Aires
(open to the public 1000-1300 only)
Tel: (1) 314 6735   Fax: (1) 314 8955

AUSTRALIA
BTA, 8th Floor,
University Centre, 210 Clarence Street,
Sydney, NSW 2000
Tel: (2) 267 4555   Fax: (2) 267 4442

BELGIUM
BTA, 306 Avenue Louise,
1050 Brussels
Tel: (2) 646 3510   Fax: (2) 646 3986

BRAZIL
BTA, Avenida Nilo Pecanha 50/1103
20044-900 Rio-de Janeiro-RJ
Tel: (21) 220 1187/7072
Fax: (21) 240 8779

CANADA
BTA, 111 Avenue Road,
Suite 450, Toronto, Ontario M5R 3J8
Tel: (416) 925 6326   Fax: (416) 961 2175

CZECH AND SLOVAK REPUBLICS
BTA, Kaprova 13, 110 01
Prague 1, PO Box 264
Tel: (2) 232 7213   Fax: (2) 232 7469

DENMARK
BTA, Møntergade 3,
1116 Copenhagen K
Tel: 33 33 91 88   Fax: 33 14 01 36

FINLAND
BTA,
Mikon Karu 13A, 00100 Helsinki
Tel: 358 9630912   Fax: 358 9622 1562

FRANCE
BTA,
Maison de la Grande-Bretagne,
19 rue des Mathurins, 75009 Paris
Tel: (1) 44 51 56 20   Fax: (1) 44 51 56 21
Minitel 3615 BRITISH

GERMANY
BTA,
Taunusstrasse 52-60,
60329 Frankfurt
Tel: (69) 2380711   Fax: (69) 2380717

HONG KONG
BTA, Room 1504,
Eton Tower, 8 Hysan Avenue,
Causeway Bay, Hong Kong
Tel: 2882 9967   Fax: 2577 1443

IRELAND
BTA,
18-19 College Green, Dublin 2
Tel: (1) 670 8000   Fax: (1) 670 8244

ITALY (Milan)
BTA,
Corso Magenta 32,
20123 Milano
Tel: (2) 7201 0078   Fax: (2) 7201 0086

ITALY (Rome)
BTA,
Corso Vittorio Emanuele 337,
00186 Rome
Tel: (6) 688 06821   Fax: (6) 687 9095

JAPAN (Osaka)
OCAT Building, 4th Floor,
1-chome, 4-1 Minatomachi, Naniwa-ku
Osaka 556
Tel: (6) 635 3093   Fax: (6) 635 3095

JAPAN (Tokyo)
BTA,
Akasaka Twin Tower IF,
2-17-22 Akasaka, Minato-ku,
Tokyo
Tel: (3) 5562 2550   Fax: (3) 5562 2551

NETHERLANDS
BTA,
Aurora Gebouw (5e),
Stadhouderskade 2, 1054 ES Amsterdam
Tel: (20) 685 50 51   Fax: (20) 618 68 68

NEW ZEALAND
BTA,
3rd Floor, Dilworth Building,
Corner Queen and Customs Streets,
Auckland 1
Tel: (9) 303 1446   Fax: (9) 377 6965

NORWAY
BTA,
Nedre Slotts Gt 21,
4 etasje, N-0157 Oslo (Visitors)
Postbox 1554 Vika, N-0117 Oslo (Mail)
Tel: (22) 42 47 45   Fax: (22) 42 48 74

PORTUGAL
BTA,
Rua Luciano Cordeiro
1232° Dr, 1050 Lisbon
Tel: (1) 312 9020 Fax: (1) 312 9030

SINGAPORE
BTA,
24 Raffles Place,
#19-06 Clifford Centre,
Singapore 048621
Tel: 535 2966   Fax: 534 4703

SOUTH AFRICA
BTA,
Lancaster Gate,
Hyde Lane, Hyde Park,
Sandton 2196 *(visitors)*
PO Box 41896, Craighall 2024
(postal address)
Tel: (11) 325 0343   Fax: (11) 325 0344

SPAIN
BTA,
Torre de Madrid 6/5,
Plaza de Espana 18, 28008, Madrid
Tel: (1) 541 13 96   Fax: (1) 542 81 49

SWEDEN
BTA, Klara Norra
Kyrkogata 29,
S 111 22 Stockholm *(visitors)*
Box 3102, 10362 Stockholm
(postal address)
Tel: (8) 4401 700   Fax: (8) 21 31 29

SWITZERLAND
(Information Office only)
BTA,
Limmatquai 78, CH-8001 Zurich
Tel: (1) 261 42 77   Fax: (1) 251 44 56

TAIWAN
BTA,
7th Floor, Fu Key Building
99 Jen Ai Road, Section 2,
Taipei 10625
Tel: (2) 351 0991   Fax: (2) 392 6653

USA (Chicago)
BTA,
625 N Michigan Avenue, Suite 1510,
Chicago IL 60611 *(personal callers only)*

USA (New York)
BTA,
551 Fifth Avenue, New York,
NY 10176-0799
Tel: 1 800 GO 2 BRITAIN
Toll free: 1-800 462 2748
Tel: (212) 986 2200
Fax: (212) 986 1188

A Brief Guide to the Welsh Language

In many parts of Wales, visitors may hear Welsh spoken as an everyday language along with English.

A few greetings

Welsh	English
Bore da	Good morning
Dydd da	Good day
Prynhawn da	Good afternoon
Noswaith dda	Good evening
Nos da	Good night
Sut mae?	How are you?
Hwyl	Cheers
Diolch	Thanks
Diolch yn fawr iawn	Thanks very much
Croeso	Welcome
Croeso i Gymru	Welcome to Wales
Da	Good
Da iawn	Very good
Iechyd da!	Good health!
Nadolig Llawen!	Merry Christmas!
Blwyddyn Newydd Dda!	Happy New Year!
Dymuniadau gorau	Best wishes
Cyfarchion	Greetings
Penblwydd hapus	Happy birthday

The Welsh National Anthem

Mae hen wlad fy nhadau yn annwyl i mi,
Gwlad beirdd a chantorion enwogion o fri;
Ei gwrol ryfelwyr, gwladgarwyr tra mad,
Dros ryddid collasant eu gwaed.
Chorus
Gwlad! Gwlad! Pleidiol wyf i'm gwlad;
Tra môr yn fur i'r bur hoff bau,
O bydded i'r hen iaith barhau.

The ancient land of my fathers is dear to me,
A land of poets and minstrels, famed men.
Her brave warriors, patriots much blessed,
It was for freedom that they lost their blood.
Chorus
Homeland! I am devoted to my country;
So long as the sea is a wall to this fair beautiful land,
May the ancient language remain.

Pronunciation

There are some sounds in spoken Welsh which are very different from their English equivalents. Here's a basic guide.

Welsh		English equivalent
c	cath (cat)	cat (never as in receive)
ch	chwaer (sister)	loch
dd	yn dda (good)	them
f	y fam (the mother)	of
ff	ffenestr (window)	off
g	gardd (garden)	garden (never as in George)
h	het (hat)	hat (never silent as in honest)
th	byth (ever)	Three (never as in the)
ll	llaw (hand)	There is no equivalent

sound. Place the tongue on the upper roof of the mouth near the upper teeth, ready to pronounce l; then blow rather than voice the l

The vowels in Welsh are a e i o u w y; all except y can be l-o-n-g or short:

long a	tad (father)	similar to hard
short a	mam (mother)	similar to ham
long e	hen (old)	similar to sane
short e	pen (head)	similar to ten
long i	mis (month)	similar to geese
short i	prin (scarce)	similar to tin
long o	môr (sea)	similar to more
short o	ffon (walking stick)	similar to fond
long w	sŵn (sound)	similar to moon
short w	gwn (gun)	similar to look

y has two sounds:

1. Clear
dyn (man) a long 'ee' sound almost like geese
cyn (before) a short 'i' sound almost like tin

2. Obscure
something like the sound in English run, eg:
y (the)
yn (in)
dynion (men)

It is well to remember that in Welsh the accent usually falls on the last syllable but one of a word, eg cadair (chair).

LLANFAIRPWLLGWYNGYLLGOGERYCHWYRNDROBWLLLLANTYSILIOGOGOGOCH
Llan-vire-pooll-guin-gill-go-ger-u-queern-drob-ooll-llandus-ilio-gogo-goch

Publications, Guides and Maps

On the next 2 pages we describe the many publications available on Wales - both saleable guides and free publications.
FOR COPIES OF ALL GUIDES AND BROCHURES (FREE AND SALEABLE), PLEASE SEE THE COUPON OPPOSITE.

'Where to Stay' guides
The official accommodation guides for Wales. All places listed have been checked out by the Wales Tourist Board. These full-colour guides also contain detailed maps and comprehensive tourist information.

Wales - Self-Catering 1997 £3.50
Thousands of self-catering properties, including cottages, flats, chalets and caravan holiday home parks. Also a huge range of parks for touring caravans, motor homes and tents.

Wales - Bed and Breakfast 1997 £3.25
See Wales on a budget with this guide. Hundreds of hotels, guest houses and farmhouses, all with one thing in common – they offer B&B for £23 or under, per person per night.

Wales Tourist Map £2.00
A best-seller – and now better than ever. Detailed 5 miles/inch scale, fully revised and updated. Also includes suggested car tours, town plans and information centres.

A Journey Through Wales £5.10

A magnificent production – 64 big-format pages of the best images in Wales. The 90 photographs take the reader on a tour of Wales's mighty castles, spectacular mountains and coastline, country towns and colourful attractions.

Wales - Castles and Historic Places £7.25
Describes more than 140 sites in full colour, including castles, abbeys, country houses, prehistoric and Roman remains. A historic introduction sets the scene, and detailed maps help visitors plan their routes.

Visitor's Guides to South, Mid and North Wales £3.55 each
Another series of best-sellers, written by Welsh author Roger Thomas. These three books give you the complete picture of Wales's holiday regions. In full colour – and packed with information.

- Descriptions of resorts, towns and villages
- Where to go and what to see
- Hundreds of attractions and places to visit
- Scenic drives, castles, crafts, what to do on a rainy day
- Detailed maps and town plans

Ghosts & Legends of Wales £5.75
144 pages of fascinating stories, ancient and modern. Some of the happenings recounted may sound incredible, many will leave the reader wondering.

Exploring Snowdonia, Anglesey and the Llŷn Peninsula £4.80

144 pages of detailed touring information, maps and illustrations. Discover the quietest roads and places to visit with this guide.

Travelmaster Guide to South Wales £8.65
New guide in the popular Jarrold Travelmaster series. Twenty car tours of South Wales plus information on what to see along the way written by author Roger Thomas. Includes the most accurate and up-to-date Ordnance Survey mapping.

'By Car' Guides   £2.40 each

- The Pembrokeshire Coast
- The Brecon Beacons

Two of the 32-page White Horse series. Attractive routes, maps and photographs – the ideal car touring guides to these beautiful parts of Wales.

Ordnance Survey Pathfinder Guides £9.65 each

- Snowdonia Walks (including Anglesey/Llŷn Peninsula)
- Pembrokeshire and Gower Walks
- Brecon Beacons and Glamorgan Walks

80-page books with detailed maps, colour illustrations and descriptions which guide you safely along attractive walking routes.

All prices include postage and packing

FREE PUBLICATIONS

Activity Wales
Magazine on all kinds of activities, from abseiling to windsurfing. Lots of information on accredited activity centres and visitor attractions, events, news and articles.

Freewheeling Cycling Breaks
See Wales on two wheels. A selection of cycling breaks and holidays, from mountain biking to leisurely routes. Accommodation and cycle hire can be arranged with just one phone call through this brochure.

Discover Wales on Horseback
Full of information on trekking and riding, with a list of accredited centres located throughout Wales, many of which also offer accommodation.

Discovering Accessible Wales (Holidays for disabled people)
A guide full of ideas and helpful information for people who may have impaired movement or are confined to a wheelchair, to enjoy with family and friends. Covers everything from accommodation to activities.

Freedom Holiday Parks Wales
Caravan Holiday Home Park accommodation in Wales is high on standards and value for money – as you'll see from this brochure which only lists parks graded for quality by the Wales Tourist Board.

Golf in Wales
Beautifully produced large-format guide to Wales's golf courses in full colour, written by Peter Corrigan, Golf Correspondent of the *Independent on Sunday*.

Wales Touring Caravan and Camping
Detailed guide to Wales Tourist Board-inspected caravan and camping parks which welcome touring caravans, motor homes and tents.

Walking Wales
A booklet on Britain's most popular leisure activity – and the best place in which to enjoy it. Suggested walks, lists of walking holiday operators and information on the countryside.

The Walled Towns of Wales and Chester
Fascinating 60-page colour guide to medieval walled towns, including Caernarfon, Conwy, Pembroke and Tenby. Historical sites plus tourist information.

PLEASE COMPLETE AND SEND TO: WALES TOURIST BOARD, DEPT HG97, DAVIS STREET, CARDIFF CF1 2FU

SALEABLE PUBLICATIONS

Please enclose the appropriate remittance in the form of a cheque (payable to Wales Tourist Board) or postal/money order in £ sterling. All prices include post and packing.

☐ Wales – Self-Catering 1997	£3.50
☐ Wales – Bed & Breakfast 1997	£3.25
☐ Wales Tourist Map	£2.00
☐ A Journey Through Wales	£5.10
☐ A Visitor's Guide to South Wales	£3.55
☐ A Visitor's Guide to Mid Wales	£3.55
☐ A Visitor's Guide to North Wales	£3.55
☐ Wales – Castles & Historic Places	£7.25
☐ Ghosts & Legends of Wales	£5.75

☐ Exploring Snowdonia, Anglesey and the Llŷn Peninsula	£4.80
☐ Travelmaster Guide to South Wales	£8.65
'By Car' Guides:	
☐ The Pembrokeshire Coast	£2.40
☐ The Brecon Beacons	£2.40
OS Pathfinder Guides:	
☐ Snowdonia Walks *(including Anglesey/Llŷn Peninsula)*	£9.65
☐ Pembrokeshire & Gower Walks	£9.65
☐ Brecon Beacons & Glamorgan Walks	£9.65

FREE PUBLICATIONS

- ☐ Activity Wales
- ☐ Freewheeling Cycling Breaks
- ☐ Discover Wales on Horseback
- ☐ Discovering Accessible Wales
- ☐ Freedom Holiday Parks Wales
- ☐ Golf in Wales
- ☐ Wales Touring Caravan & Camping
- ☐ Walking Wales
- ☐ The Walled Towns of Wales & Chester

Name *(please print)*: ....

Address *(please print)*: ....

....Post Code: ....

Total remittance enclosed *(if applicable)*: £ ....   Cheque *(payable to Wales Tourist Board)* /PO or Money Order No *(if applicable)*: ....

Maps of Wales

The maps which follow divide Wales into 12 sections, each with a slight overlap. The grid overlaying each map will help you find the resort, town or village of your choice. Please refer to the map and grid reference which appears alongside the name of each place listed in the 'Where to Stay' gazetteers.

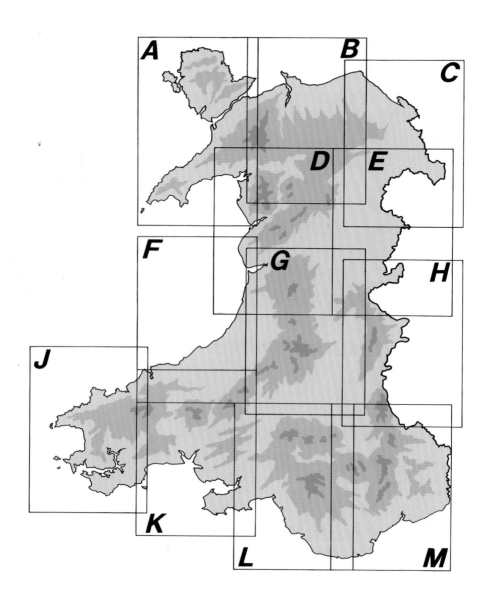

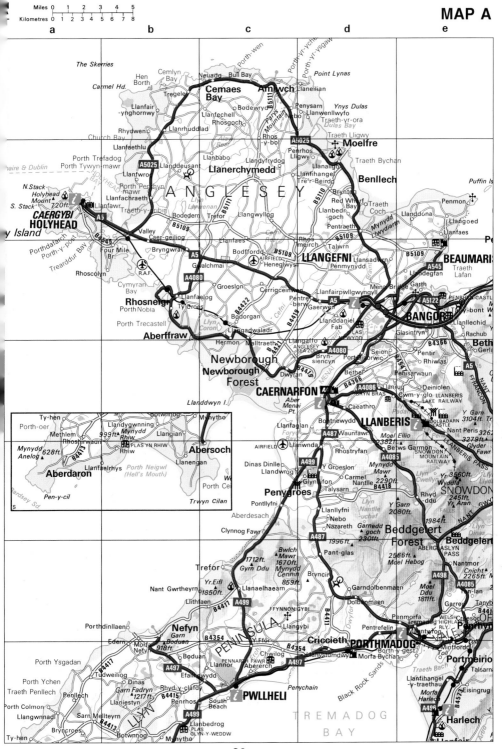

MAP B

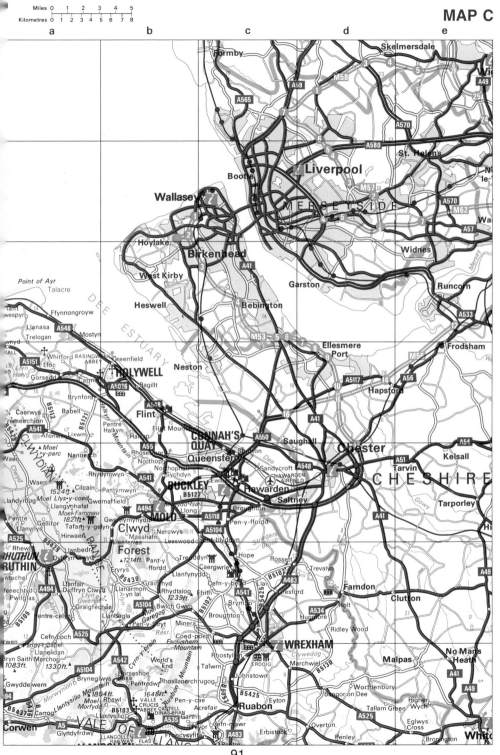

MAP C

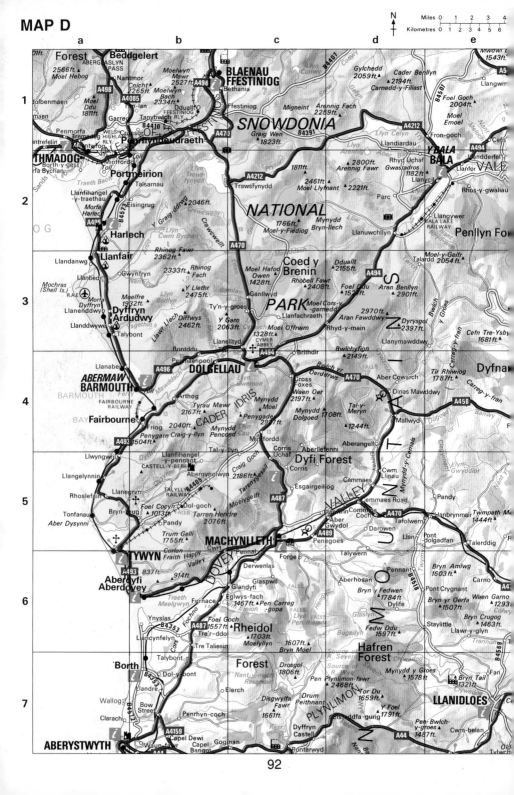

MAP D

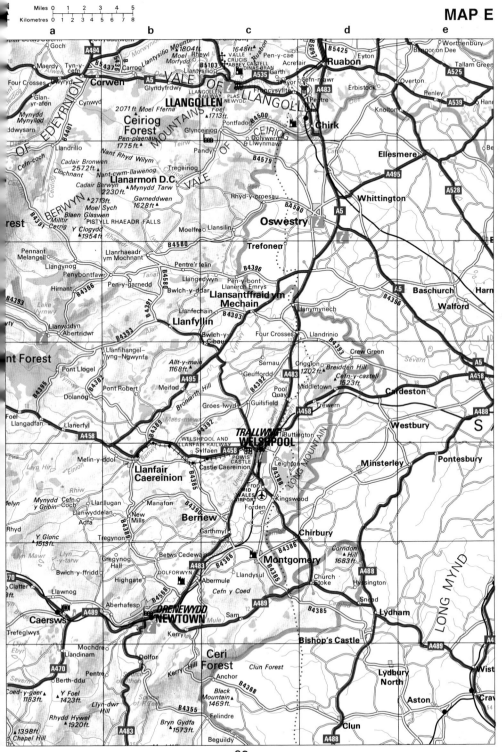

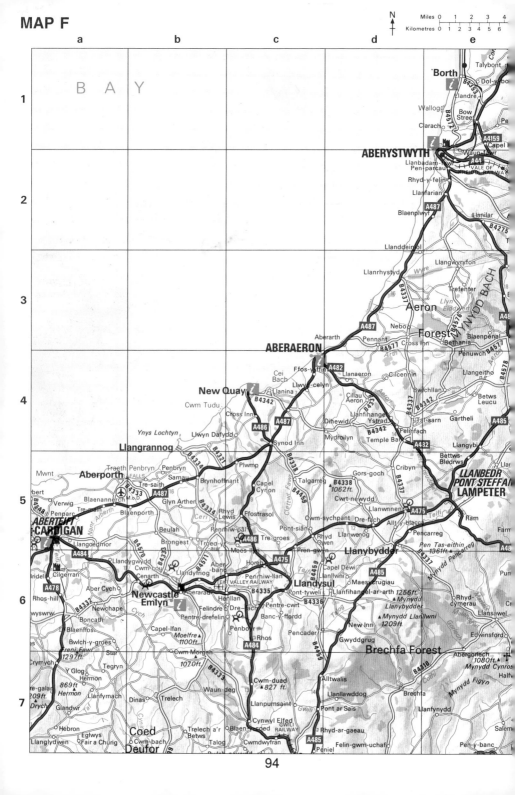

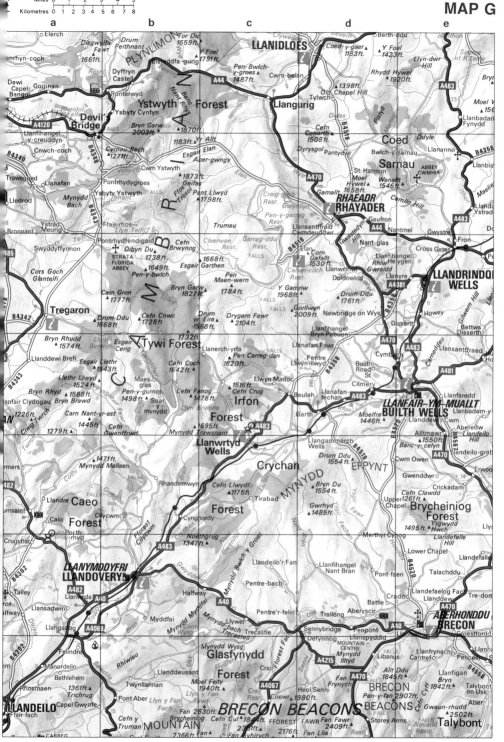

95

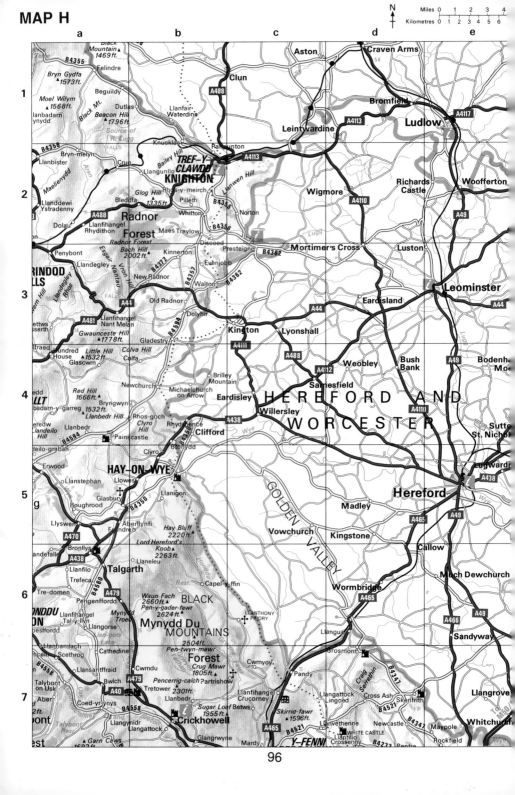

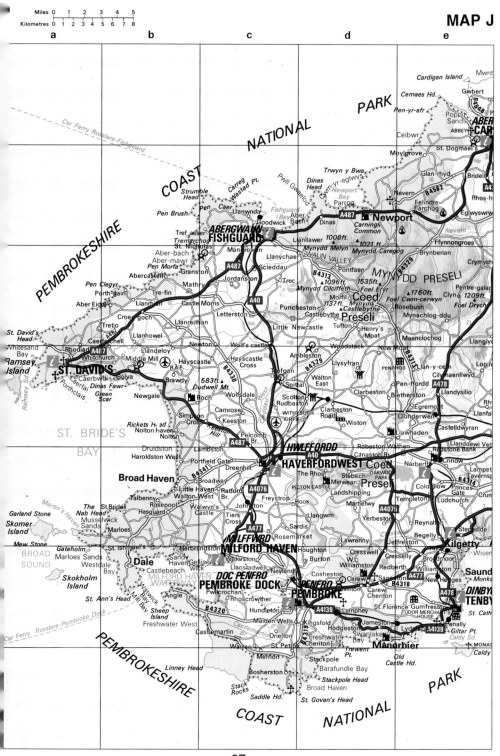

MAP K

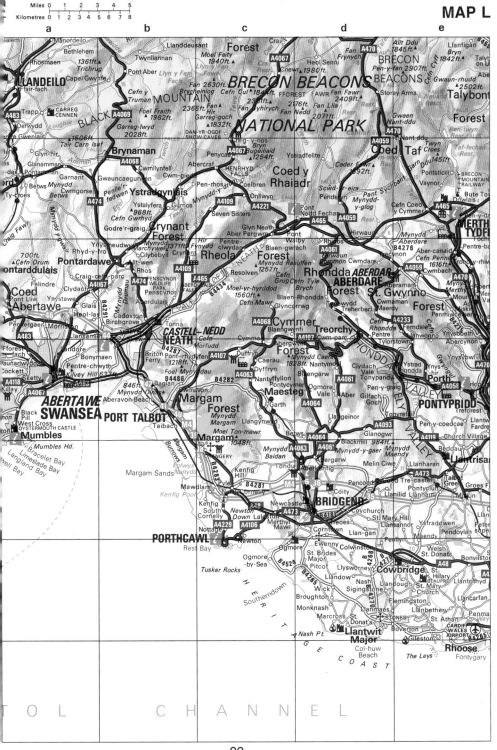

MAP L

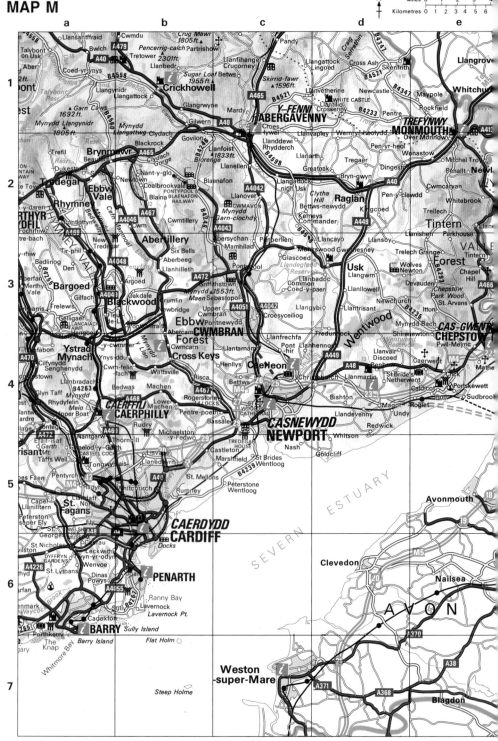